WESTMAR COLLEGE LIBRARY

W9-BWZ-941

Government and Politics in the Twentieth Century

REVISED EDITION

By Gwendolen M. Carter
and John H. Herz

FREDERICK A. PRAEGER, *Publishers*
New York · Washington

JA
66
.C3
1965

BOOKS THAT MATTER

Published in the United States of America in 1965
by Frederick A. Praeger, Inc., Publishers
111 Fourth Avenue, New York 3, N. Y.

This is a new and completely revised edition of a book first published
in 1961 by Frederick A. Praeger, Inc.

All rights reserved

© 1961, 1965 by Frederick A. Praeger, Inc.
Library of Congress Catalog Card Number: 65–25402

Portions of this book have been adapted, and some short passages
reprinted, with permission, from the concluding section, Part V, of
Major Foreign Powers, 3d edition, © 1957 by Harcourt, Brace & World

Printed in the United States of America

63824

PREFACE

The systematic study of comparative government and politics has commonly been concerned only with the institutions and activities of European countries and the United States. Moreover, in the still relatively rare works in which the institutions of the newer countries have been examined analytically, the consideration has nearly always been either of a particular state or of several of these states compared with each other. This book seeks to broaden the focus of comparative analysis by dealing with both developed and developing countries and by testing generalizations obtained from the study of mature states in the light of the experience of the newer states of Asia, Africa, the Middle East, and Latin America.

Accepting the dichotomy of democracy and totalitarianism, we recognize that even highly developed states do not conform exactly to the characteristic features of either system. Particularly among the newer states there are political systems which lie between democracy and totalitarianism, not only partaking of the characteristics of both, but also adding something distinctive of their own.

This book makes no pretense at finality. Rather, we have sought to stimulate further investigation into a field which becomes increasingly suggestive as its focus is widened. We have therefore deliberately sought great breadth of scope. We have been concerned with the operation and results in different settings of what may seem to be similar institutions, with those forces which make for uniformity and those which make for diversity, with the interaction of traditional and revolutionary forces, and with reactions to the strains of ideological conflict and cold war. While putting into sharp focus the divergencies of governmental and political systems in the twentieth-century world, and while not playing down the conflict situations which such divergency is bound to create, we hope also to have made clear the merit which can exist in systems that differ from Western democracy. It is in accordance with the democratic approach, whose validity we affirm, to grant others their right to find their own institutional answers to their particular problems. Only thus can this "one world" become a world of neighbors.

GWENDOLEN M. CARTER
JOHN H. HERZ

PREFACE TO SECOND EDITION

When this small volume was first published four years ago, it evoked a degree of interest both in this country and abroad (evidenced by its translation into seven foreign languages) which was as exhilarating as it was unexpected. In bringing out this new edition we wish to express our appreciation above all to those of our critics who have taken us to task for occasional lack of clarity and precision of definition. We have tried to cope with these shortcomings by placing systems and institutions into what we believe to be a clearer and more adequate conceptional framework. We hope that these remedies, plus the numerous and at times comprehensive changes in detail which, in a book like this, are necessitated by new developments and emphases, will render this volume a more useful one.

GWENDOLEN M. CARTER
JOHN H. HERZ

July, 1965

CONTENTS

vii

Government
and
Politics in the
Twentieth
Century

I

THE ROLE OF GOVERNMENT IN CONTEMPORARY SOCIETY

The author of the first great treatise on government and politics known to history found it necessary to analyze, compare, and contrast more than one hundred and fifty polities and their constitutions as a basis for his conclusions. A present-day Aristotle would have to do at least as much to speak with any hope of realism of government and politics in the twentieth-century world. Compared with the range of political systems in the relatively close world of the ancient polis, that of current political units all over the world seems, indeed, to be vastly broader. Its diversity becomes apparent when one contrasts systems not only in the so-called "free" world with those of totalitarian dictatorships, but also those within each of these groups. There is especially great variety among the former, but significant differences have more recently become noticeable even among the latter. In addition, there is the heritage of premodern countries and their traditional value systems and political ways of life. And this heritage, while its liquidation is on the agenda of our times, still affects not only the internal affairs of the areas concerned, but also their relations with the modern world, as is attested by the sometimes promising, but occasionally tragic story of their entrance as independent units into this modern world.

MODERNIZATION AND MODERN GOVERNMENT

This participation by all states in a common process of "development" is as inevitable as it is relentless. Mankind has

3

entered upon the age of "modernity," with its one-directional sweep based on the values and findings of science and technology. This age is characterized by a universal desire for the fruits of affluence and, as a result, by a type of uniformity that renders the different groups and civilizations of mankind ever more devoid of distinct and distinctive features. The end result may even be a homogeneous mankind, with its abundantly diverse forms of culture and civilization and its widely varied stages of development merged into a controlled, organized, and largely man-made cosmos.

In these conditions, government, the chief agency of such control, is likely to emerge as a more and more vital instrumentality of "modernization." The technological process itself is characterized by an accelerating rate of change and in turn produces ever more rapid changes throughout society and human affairs. Coupled with the population explosion (especially in the developing countries) and the increasingly rapid move of the masses to metropolitan areas, it poses entirely new, and, in the case of the not-yet-modernized countries, almost insuperable tasks to government. Other, equally vital, tasks are created by the headlong rush toward "control of nature," through which man's natural habitat is being destroyed in favor of a synthetic environment. Here, the rate of change is particularly remarkable, and potentially dangerous. It took man thousands of years to gain insight into the nature of his environment and to evolve means of survival in his struggle with hostile forces (such as wild animals). It took only hundreds of years to discover all of the globe and to explore it. Now man is propelling himself into the universe, reaching for the moon and beyond, and at the same time transforming the surface of the earth itself into "cultivated" areas, producing an artificial "second nature" directly and exclusively serving the maintenance of humans—indeed one huge factory providing the necessities of life on the pattern of the synthetic environment provided for the inhabitants of spacecraft.

Obviously, the ensuing problems of the preservation of resources, natural as well as human, of land and landscape, purity of water and air, and the protection of physical health, endangered as it is by pollution and chemicals, and of mental health, threatened by the "modern" mechanized way of life, test the ingenuity of organized society. It is equally clear that many, perhaps most, of these tasks can no longer be performed by individuals and smaller groups but must be undertaken by the "Great Society," even, increasingly, through the cooperation of such societies, i.e., of countries and their governments on a regional or global level.

Thus, the distinguishing feature of modern government is its universal recognition and acceptance as an active force in the forming of economic, social, and environmental conditions. Even the most reluctant take this process more and more for granted. While the idea that government should be only an umpire adjudicating the rules by which other forces in society compete still commands greater allegiance in the United States than in Great Britain or in France, even this country accepts with little question such governmental activities as the TVA or credit controls or the increasing amount of direct government intervention to cope with such problems of modernization as facilities and transportation in vast urban complexes and the elimination of "poverty in the midst of plenty." Moreover, the United States' major political and ideological opponent, the Soviet Union, which in theory is so antagonistic and different in outlook and structure, shares fully and even enthusiastically the underlying ideal and attitude of "modernity." In fact, one of its major stated objectives is to "match and surpass" the United States technologically, scientifically, and economically, areas which, in Communist societies, of course, are entirely the responsibility of the state.

Modernity is, above all, the ideal and the fervently held aim of the "emerging," "developing" areas (once described as "backward" and "underdeveloped") which, as the acceptable words themselves indicate, now define themselves wholly in terms of the one-directional movement toward this higher standard of technical proficiency and material results. A touching, almost religious faith in the necessity, inevitability, and indeed superiority of modernity lies behind the efforts of that rising part of mankind. Thus, in the older democracies, and still more in the newer developing states as well as in the Communist countries, government is looked on as a major, or even the dominant, organizing power in society.

THE RISE OF THE MODERN STATE

So much have we become accustomed to the idea of government as an active, positive agent in the direction of the affairs of our communities that we often fail to realize the significance of the change this idea represents. In the English-speaking countries particularly, the nineteenth-century view was that government should restrict itself to the basic, and somewhat negative, function of maintaining law and order, acting only, as the half-contemptuous phrase expresses it, as a "night watchman." The transformation of this concept of the state into the modern concept of the welfare or social-service state is indeed a revolution.

This transformation in the role of the state is in essence a by-product of economic and social changes which are themselves of revolutionary character. The French Revolution and the industrial revolution—two separate but nevertheless inescapably interrelated historical forces—gave rise to a profound change in attitudes toward the individual and his place within the community. The French Revolution preached the equality of individuals, a doctrine which directly challenged the long-existent, rigid social hierarchies of Europe; at the same time, it aroused the sentiment of nationalism which exalts the community. Thus, the individual was freed, only to be merged into the group. But if the French Revolution provided much of the ideology and spur for social change, it was the industrial revolution which provided the new circumstances in which change was inevitable. Industrialism, with its new modes of production, opened the way for individual activity and permitted social mobility to a degree never before seen. Yet, while industrialism stimulated individualism, particularly in its early stages, its own inner logic was toward mass production, standardization, and vast economic units. Thus with industrialization as with the French Revolution, the tendency was to free the individual from the restrictions of the past only to fit him into new and larger entities. Inevitably, the breakdown of traditional social and economic groupings produced the mass society characteristic of our time. This mass society, as we have seen, is now undergoing the process of accelerated change that is called "modernization," the "scientific-technological revolution," or, in the field of economy, the "second industrial revolution," based on computerized services and planning and on automation. This process with its array of new tasks and problems, inevitably enhances the role of the state.

It is a strange paradox that the two chief theories produced during, and in consequence of, the age of industrialization, namely Marxism and liberalism, were both based on expectations in the political field that proved the opposite of what ensued in practice. The one forecast the "withering away" of the state, the other, its reduction to insignificance under conditions of *"laissez faire."* In contrast, what developed was either totalitarianism or the rise of the giant welfare—and all too often warfare—state.

Both these nineteenth-century theories simply failed to reckon with, or even to anticipate, the incredible technological potentialities for domination in the twentieth century. Although wholly negative and destructive use has been made of these potentialities through the annihilation and exploitation machines of Hitler and of Stalin, they can equally be used for constructive purposes. In either case, however, their effects are too far-reaching to permit them to be exercised outside the control of the state. The nuclear weapon on one side, and "atoms for peace" on the other are merely the current ultimates in the vast range of these powers and capabilities. There are others, frequently overlooked, which are equally, if not more, foreboding or promising. Science reveals more and more the mental and social malleability of man in mass society, and even the feasibility of biological transformation. This fact opens vistas of psychological manipulation and eugenic determination of inheritance that might change the very substance of man and mankind. If the state does—and perhaps must—control such decisive actions, who or what controls, or restrains, the state? Perhaps we already know too much for the safety of mankind. Since knowledge is power, the predominant problem becomes one of restraint, of limits and limitations. More than ever before, therefore, the problem of limited power, one of the major themes in our subsequent analysis, emerges as perhaps *the* foremost problem both of political science and of political practice.

BIG AND ACTIVE GOVERNMENT

In the new mass society, the role of government—the complex of institutions that have a monopoly of organized force in internal and external affairs—of necessity has changed. The state, the organized political community, needs a certain degree of stability in the social system in order to maintain its own equilibrium; this requires not only the adjustment of conflicting demands by different groups in the new social and economic order, but also the deliberate creation of conditions of social well-being demanded by the new doctrine of equality.

Thus, government, as the agent of the state, has been forced more and more to assume positive responsibility for the creation and distribution of wealth. In so doing, it has almost universally become big government, both in scope and in the numbers of those employed in carrying on its responsibilities.

There are two chief problems arising from this development. In the first place, a greatly increased number of persons become government officials and, thus, peculiarly subject to the pressures of an unscrupulous regime. In some Western countries, the state pays the salaries not only of those carrying on the public administration at the local as well as national level, but also of all those engaged in public education and even—through taxation, as with the churches in Germany—of the clergy. Democratic countries erect safeguards, such as merit and classification systems, and in France there is the highly effective Council of State, to protect public employees against favoritism in appointment and promotions, undue influence, or exploitation. It was not difficult, however, for the Hitler regime (to take but one example) to disregard many of these protective devices and use to the full the influence afforded by the unusually large number of public employees in Germany.

More serious, under normal conditions, is the problem of concentration of power, particularly power over the economy in a highly developed state. The struggle to improve living conditions has led all advanced states to undertake a substantial amount of public regulation of the economy and an increasing degree of economic planning. It is often argued that to subject the expert planners to control by the inexpert public would destroy the value of their plans. Moreover, planning requires a firm and stable government, it is said, for no plan can be effective if its sponsors are likely to be turned out of office at any moment and their policies reversed, or even if important modifications can be made by parliamentary vote. And while it is not difficult to point out that, in practice, democracies have erected safeguards in this field, too, such as decentralization through the public corporation, the very complexity and far-reaching character of the operations which government now undertakes can leave no one feeling entirely complacent about the degree to which popular control of public activities is possible. Add to this the almost incredible intrusions which government agencies can now make into the most intimate spheres of one's personal life—e.g., "bugging" a home or place of work through electronic devices—and one arrives at an uncomfortably close parallel of government and the Big Brother of Orwell's counterutopia, *Nineteen Eighty-four*.

Thus, keeping government in the twentieth-century world responsible and yet effective places a tremendous strain both on the machinery and personnel of government as well as on the alertness and active concern of the public and its organs of information. In this respect, the age-old problem of responsiveness to public opinion vs. manipulation of opinion has been rendered immeasurably more difficult by the growing complexity of issues inherent in the process and age of "modernization." There is an ever-increasing complexity in technical matters (Who, for instance, understands or even knows the technicalities of military defense and defense systems?), in the economic sphere (Who feels at home with the technicalities of a large-scale national budget or of the international payments problems?), and in organizational affairs (Who understands the structure of even one of the large executive agencies of the U.S. Government, let alone the overlapping setups in totalitarian countries?). Moreover, the public is daily confronted with (or fails to face) an increasing number of issues. And there is the growing size of the group whose attitudes and views should be taken into consideration by the policy-makers who are supposed to be responsive to the public.

From all these facts and difficulties, some observers have drawn the conclusion that an authoritarian government, able to act promptly and decisively without regard to special pressures, constitutional obstacles, or the need to conciliate mass opinion, is more efficient and far better suited to the conditions of modern government than is a democracy. We can point out in return that in two world wars, democracies proved able to mobilize their resources as efficiently, if not quite as quickly, as dictatorships, and that the more mature democracies have been able to provide higher standards of living for their people than have any dictatorships, though this is partly because of the wealth of their resources and their advantage in having had an earlier start. But as we watch the progressive industrialization of the newer countries, we must be aware that one of their greatest difficulties will be so to handle their governmental machinery that it performs expertly the tasks which they ask of it and, at the same time, remains responsible and responsive to the interests of the public which it serves.

II

DEMOCRACY AND TOTALITARIANISM: POLAR POINTS IN THE POLITICAL SPECTRUM

Although all modern governments today exercise a wide range of responsibilities, there remain highly significant differences between the objectives and techniques of those states which we call democratic and those which are avowedly totalitarian, whether of the Communist or fascist type. Democracy and totalitarianism as systems form polar points on the spectrum of political alternatives. At the same time, there is a wide range of governmental forms between the two which do not fit neatly into either category.

In order to distinguish between, and clearly categorize, forms of polities, analysis should proceed in terms of a twofold dichotomy, depending on which one of the two most fundamental questions is posed.

The first question concerns the subject, or "bearer" of political rule: Who governs? To this the answer may be: the totality of the adult members of a particular political community, i.e., "the people." In that case, we call this form of government "democracy." If the answer is only one, or a few, or an elite, or some type of minority, we call this regime "rule from above." More specifically, it can be categorized as an absolute monarchy or a one-man dictatorship or an oligarchy, aristocracy, or authoritarian system.

Quite different are the answers to the second basic question which may be posed in regard to government, and which concerns the spheres controlled by political authority of whatever type. How wide is this sphere? Here the two polar answers are either that political authority is exercised in principle over everything in the life of the respective people and society, in which case we refer to the regime as "totalitarian," or that government is limited, leaving certain, often large, spheres of individual and group life unregulated. If these spheres are guaranteed by law or protected by convention against government intervention, we refer to the regime as "liberal."

Definitions such as these are subject to historical change and qualification. The "people," who in terms of Greek antiquity constituted the bearers of a "democratic" system (Athenian democracy) today would be considered the rulers of an oligarchic system, lording it over a majority of slaves, noncitizens, and women. Most people today would refuse to characterize the rule of the white minority in South Africa as "democratic," a designation accorded it in the past (or, as far as local and state matters are concerned, to the rule exercised in Mississippi and other restrictive areas in the southern United States). Equally, to a *laissez faire* liberal of the mid-nineteenth century (and to those who still echo their views), the degree of government regulation and government intervention, especially in the fields of economy and industrial relations, which obtains today in "liberal-democratic" countries such as the United States, would certainly have appeared as "totalitarian." While we should be sensitive to these changes of view and of definitions at different periods of history, our task is to give them content in terms of current needs and conditions.

How then do these pairs of concepts and systems correlate? Theoretically, each could correlate to any one of the others, e.g., liberalism to democracy yet also to oligarchy or aristocracy, totalitarianism to dictatorship yet also to democracy. Indeed, there are historical examples, if only incidentally, of such seemingly "incongruous" pairing. Especially in the initial stages of a popular revolution, democracy can tend to disregard limitations on political authority and thus be "totalitarian." Authoritarian rule may at times be restrained by the acceptance of limitations (which are at times even constitutional ones), as witness the early nineteenth-century monarchical-aristocratic "constitutionalism" of continental European countries, or of England before it became fully democratic. De Gaulle's France may be a contemporary example.

Much more common, however, both historically and organizationally, is the pairing of the two other characteristics resulting in liberal democracy, on the one hand, and totalitarian dictatorship (or totalitarian oligarchy) on the other. Experience suggests, in fact, that totalitarian democracy, as in the French Revolution, tends to turn into small-group or one-man rule, while a liberal authoritarianism, such as existed in many earlier European regimes, tends to give way to full-fledged liberal democracy. The combination of liberalism and democracy characterized political developments in the Western countries during the era encompassing the rise of the middle classes and the first industrial revolution, i.e., roughly, the eighteenth and nineteenth centuries. In the twentieth century, the United States, Great Britain, and the first overseas members of the Commonwealth of Nations—Canada, Australia and New Zealand—and most of the countries of Western Europe, successfully adapted liberal democracy to new social and economic demands. Elsewhere, however, the impact of unsolved social and international problems created a reaction that turned many societies into totalitarian ones, politically controlled by dictatorship. This development reached its acme in the fascism of the German-Nazi variety and in the Stalinist version of Communism.

Between these polar-type regimes are many others that more or less approximate totalitarian dictatorship, and at least as many that "more or less" approximate liberal democracy. Certain regimes characterized by dictatorial or oligarchic controls may lack some or most of the characteristics of totalitarianism. In fact, the standard, traditional forms of "rule from above," as they are inherited from the predemocratic, more or less authoritarian past, still prevail in many countries of the not-yet-modernized variety, as, for example, in traditional Latin American junta rule. As we shall see, many of the newly independent countries of Africa and Asia also seem to go through at least a period of authoritarianism or even dictatorship, without embracing full-fledged totalitarianism.

Despite individual variants, the norms are sufficiently constant so that in contrasting, in the following pages, democracy and totalitarianism as the chief polar opposites of political and governmental structures, we shall use our terms in the following ways: unless otherwise noted, we shall use the term "democracy" in the sense of "liberal democracy," and the term "totalitarianism" in the sense of "totalitarian dictatorship" or "totalitarian oligarchy."

At the same time, it should be understood that both systems and concepts are "relative" ones, each differing in character not only between countries, but also between stages of development. Thus, totalitarian states differ in revolutionary fervor, in type of leadership, in organization of social and economic structure, and, as has become increasingly clear in recent years, in degree of "total" or not quite total controls. On the other hand, even mature democracies sometimes exhibit, particularly in periods of crisis, some of the characteristics of totalitarianism; the dictatorial powers given to democratic executives in time of war (e.g., Great Britain in both world wars) are cases in point. But what proved the chief democratic safeguard even in such instances was the universal agreement, or common consensus, that such powers were granted temporarily, and that control would be reassumed by the "people" through its customary channels and representatives as soon as the emergency was over. In cases, however, where those to whom such temporary controls are entrusted abuse them to continue their "emergency powers" indefinitely, liberal democracy degenerates into autocracy.

Despite all these gradations and transitions, there exist clearly definable features of democracy and totalitarianism which sharply distinguish the two. These features can be identified and used as standards for testing the character and operations of governmental and political systems, for the differences between them are not only institutional but also go back to basic world-views and attitudes.

CHARACTERISTICS OF DEMOCRACIES

Liberal democracies are characterized institutionally by limitations on governmental action to provide safeguards for individuals and groups, by means for securing the regular, periodic, and peaceful change of their leaders, and by organs of effective popular representation. In attitude, they require tolerance for opposing opinions, flexibility, and willingness for experimentation. Limitation on governmental actions means not only that there are private spheres of life in which government must not interfere, but also that governmental agents, like private persons, must abide by the rules of law and exercise authority only to the degree the law provides. Peaceful changes of representation and of leaders involve a system of elections with some genuine measure of choice between candidates, either at the nomination or the election level. It implies a system of nomination and also a formulation of program which is associated with the candidates who are running for office. It necessitates political organization, commonly in the form of political parties, to keep constant contact between the public and its leaders and representatives. Moreover, so that choice may be exercised freely and public policies kept under review, political parties and other associations must have the opportunity openly to analyze issues, criticize governmental actions, and crystallize public sentiment. Organs of opinion—the press, radio, and TV—must be permitted the independent purveyance of news and formulation of judgments. Thus, freedom of speech, of association, and of assembly are essential political as well as civil rights.

To make democracy effective, however, requires not only institutions and guarantees, but also attitudes. Respect for the right of the people to assert their point of view, however unpopular or seemingly wrong-headed, is fundamental to the workings of the democratic process of discussion and choice. This basic attitude is expressed in the saying, "I abhor your opinion, but I shall fight to the death for your right to express it." Nothing can exert a greater influence on the democratic character of a state than the individual citizen's tolerance of (though not indifference to) ideas, whether expressed individually or through associations, which are contrary to or challenge his own. Censorship and governmental restraint are obvious ways of creating conformism, but social pressure may be no less a force in crushing the interplay of ideas on which democracy depends.

Democracy is characterized further by respect for minority and individual rights, by the use of discussion rather than force to settle disputes, by an acceptance of the legitimacy of the system under which the people are governed, and by the experimental method. Democracies have ideals and objectives, but they do not have fixed goals. Thus they proceed through trial and error, changing their programs in response to popular need and present circumstance. All states are limited by their past and by their environment, but democracies believe that they are not restricted by any inevitable process of history and that there exist opportunities for experiment and choice of alternatives.

THE NATURE OF TOTALITARIANISM

In contrast to the conscious efforts of democracies to maintain diversity, open discussion, freedom of choice among ideas and leaders, and open-mindedness on future programs, totalitarianism is characterized by a persistent drive to enforce unity, by the crushing of open opposition, and by a leadership which claims superior, if not infallible knowledge of how policy should be directed and which exercises power through a self-perpetuating elite. Behind these actions lies an ideology or doctrine which justifies the concentration of power—and whatever restrictions on individual and group liberties this involves —as the means necessary to attain some ultimate and fixed goal or certain end toward which nature or history are said to strive.

Communist Totalitarianism

Thus, Communism, for instance, not only as seen from outside but even more in its self-interpretation, is very different from simple rule by force or autocracy. Because everything which happens now is meant to be merely a transitional stage on history's inexorable path toward a future depicted as one of complete human emancipation and freedom, everything, be it ever so coercive, partakes of the nature of a necessary but minor evil to attain this end. Opinion has to be controlled and censorship instituted; but this is only because portions of the public are still "backward" in their "social consciousness," and therefore have to be "educated" by a "vanguard" which possesses full consciousness of history and the things to come. This same vanguard has to exercise controls and accumulate powers which, to the uninitiated, look excessive and dictatorial; but the holders of power consider themselves the agents of a movement which fulfills the deepest yearnings of the masses of the people, and therefore purport to act "democratically" in a more profound way than do the people's representatives in the West who, according to this view, are merely self-seeking agents or stooges of business and other "interests."

Thus, Communist leaders, in their own view, are performing the historic task of social and general reconstruction, a task which ennobles whatever shortcomings the current Eastern-style "democracies" may still embody. If East Berlin, for instance, appears shoddy to a Western visitor who contrasts it to the Western part of the city, it does not seem so to a person steeped in the "right" philosophy; to the latter, any building or enterprise owned "by the people" is intrinsically superior to the glittering façade of a structure which, because capitalist-owned, symbolizes the degeneracy of the capitalist system. Moreover, the former is bound, in due course, to surpass the latter, even in aesthetic terms, and thus will attain the beauty of the "higher system" which the true believer already discerns in what is defective at present.

It is a basic characteristic of Communism that it makes social change a major objective and that it mobilizes all the instruments of the modern industrialized state—technology, education, communication media—to accelerate this process. In doing so, it has a twofold objective: to move as rapidly as possible toward the transcendent goals which are formulated by its leaders, and to keep the society so mobile that nonparty groups have little chance to stabilize and thus exercise effective influence on its character. Thus, what is often called "permanent revolution" characterizes these regimes. The early Soviet Five-Year Plans were major instruments of social and economic revolution backed by fear, force, and measurable, though often unattainable, production goals. Moreover, in the background of all totalitarian regimes—and sometimes in the foreground—is the purge: a technique of government with its own positive as well as negative features.

The purge promotes specific policies at the same time that it removes those who oppose them. It may eliminate, displace, or undercut the power of those against whom it is aimed. It acts against those considered a danger to the ruling elite either because they hold different social objectives (as was true of sizable groups in the early days of fascist and Communist regimes) or because they endorse different techniques for moving toward the common goal (as did those in the Soviet Union who, in the 1920's and again in early post-Stalinist days, emphasized the need for consumers goods rather than the concentration on heavy industry) or because they threaten to establish the predominant influence of a nonparty group (as in Hitler's purges of the military, and Khrushchev's replacing by party control the influence of the so-called economic bureaucracy, the managers of state-owned industry, over production and distribution in their own segments of the economy).

Fascist Totalitarianism

It may perhaps be questioned whether the Nazi system, though totalitarian in its use of the purge and in its total interference—in theory as well as practice—with all spheres of life and society, also shared the other characteristic of Communist totalitarian regimes: their social and economic dynamism. Initially, the Hitler regime did not affect such established institutions as business enterprises and private property; through steadily increasing control of economic as well as all other matters, it tended more and more, however, to deprive such institutions of their usual functions. Of what use were private holdings, in practice, when all discretion of the holder to plan production, employ labor, and determine wage and price policies was taken away through over-all control by planning agencies, which, in turn, were dependent on the varying policies of the political leadership? And, particularly, of what use were they when the holder, like any other individual, might at any time disappear in a concentration camp in case he failed to comply? Hitler himself once commented that there was no need to socialize the means through which business and commerce were carried on, since "we socialize human beings." In addition, Nazism showed signs in its later stages of carrying through a more radical transformation of the economic and social structure, and it may be doubted whether capitalism—or any other traditional system or structure—could have endured if the Nazi system itself had lasted.

Nazism provides the most extreme case of fascist totalitarianism. In comparison with Nazism, other fascist regimes, including the one that furnished its name, Italian Fascism, not only were, or are, less "totalitarian" in their intended or actual control of spheres of life and society, but frequently less dynamic also. Italian Fascism, as one of its early critics put it, had risen as a "counterrevolution against a revolution that never took place"; throughout its tenure, it seemed intent on preserving basic institutions of the economy and society. Indeed, it did not even destroy such traditional political institutions as the monarchy, powerless though it rendered it. Other fascist, or proto-fascist regimes, such as those in Spain and Portugal, have proved even more conservative and traditionalist. In some instances, as in the case of Franco Spain and that of the dictatorship of "Admiral" Horthy in Hungary, the dictators officially proclaim their rule as a regency for a vanished or to-be-re-established monarchy. Such versions of totalitarianism or dictatorship thus actually came close to what Marxian interpretation says of any and all "fascism": that it constitutes the rule of traditional forces such as "monopoly capitalism." In reality, this type of dictatorship is more frequently powered by non-middle class groups, such as the church and landed aristocracy, which eliminate liberal democracy for fear the latter will prove too weak to withstand the onslaught of revolutionary proletarian forces.

Such regimes, then, may turn out to be replicas of traditional, pre-democratic "authoritarian" regimes, not unlike

Latin American military or junta control. They strive to maintain one-man or oligarchic control in a community without basically changing its structure. They tend to preserve the traditional social structure and to work through established lines of authority. As a means of maintaining their dominance, they aim at preserving a climate of internal tranquility quite unlike the climate of permanent change and dynamic transformation prevailing in the full-fledged totalitarian regimes. While it is going too far to speak of General Charles de Gaulle's administration in the Fifth French Republic as being such a system, its aim certainly has been similar, namely, to reduce tensions, prevent social revolution, and establish governmental stability. One over-all problem facing such regimes is whether their political conservatism can withstand the "winds of change" which modernization—the aim of all or most countries—carries with it. A predemocratic climate of attitudes, especially in the relationship between governors and governed, is ill suited to the antipaternalistic tendencies of "modern" man in the modernized, technically oriented machine world.

DEVELOPING STATES BETWEEN DEMOCRACY AND TOTALITARIANISM

In contrast to the more or less genuinely reactionary regimes, rapid social and economic change is the objective not only of totalitarian states, but also of many of the new, developing countries of Asia, Africa, and the Middle East which are striving to achieve modernity in record time. Their leaders face an obvious temptation to adopt totalitarian techniques to achieve this difficult purpose. Yet the appeals of totalitarianism are counterbalanced by its price. Totalitarianism demands a radical reorganization of society, which has its heaviest impact on the landed peasantry, the base of all underdeveloped countries. It tends to make the power structure rigid at a time when new national leaders seek to give their people a feeling of participation in the exercise of authority and thereby to legitimize their claims to supersede traditional authorities. It limits their opportunities to secure aid from the West as well as the East when most of them prefer to remain uncommitted to either.

For these reasons, the leaders of developing countries often attempt to combine features of both democratic and totalitarian systems. They organize state-directed community action at the same time that they foster individual enterprise. They favor one-party regimes without, however, crushing opportunities for individual or group opposition to particular programs or techniques. They sometimes incorporate the opposition, as in Guinea and Kenya, rather than eliminate it by force. They attempt to secure majority or even universal support by the popularity of their efforts to promote national growth and international recognition. As in India, they maintain the flexibility and experimental approach which are characteristically democratic at the same time that they race ahead with far-reaching economic projects.

No one can say with assurance whether the developing states will be able to establish the framework of stability within which flexible change most fruitfully takes place; whether they can establish the norms of action which underpin the authority of administrators; and whether they can transform traditional societies through persuasion rather than compulsion. Many people deny that democracy is suitable, or even feasible, for societies with low levels of literacy, minimal standards of living for the bulk of their people, and few resources. These comments can be better evaluated after the more careful study of systems of government and the workings of institutions to which much of this book is devoted. It is worth noting here, however, that the leaders of many of the developing states believe their states are and will remain democratic, and are working for this objective.

Is Democracy Adequate for
Modern Conditions?

While some people believe that only mature countries like Great Britain, the United States, Canada, or Sweden can maintain democracy under current conditions of international strain and the competition of totalitarian states, others question whether democracy is a workable system even for the Anglo-Saxon and European states that have been most successful in practicing it in the past. They maintain that its machinery is inadequate to modern needs. They assert that democracy's assumptions about tolerance, discussion, responsible leadership, and willingness to experiment are based on an unrealistic expectation of rationality and maturity on the part of ordinary individuals and, more particularly, of their leaders. And they affirm further that the totalitarian ideology has a more compelling attraction than has democracy in the relatively rootless, industrialized, and urbanized society of today. These criticisms of, and doubts about, democracy thus fall into three categories: the adequacy of its machinery; the assumptions it makes about human capacities; and the strength of its appeal in an age of uncertainty and tension. In addition, these same people query democracy's capacity to deal effectively with foreign affairs in the nuclear age, a problem which will be taken up later on.

Is Its Machinery Suitable?

As to the machinery of democracy, it is questioned whether executives can be decisive and far-sighted at the same time that they are responsible to the public. Moreover, can democratic leaders afford to be influenced by what are perhaps passing currents of opinion, it is asked, when the issues they deal with affect such all-important questions as national security? In addition, can the public be trusted to select for the chief offices of state persons who possess judgment and capacities of leadership? In other words, is there not a basic inconsistency in the notion that efficiency can be combined with responsibleness? If it is said in answer that elected leaders provide the responsible element in a democracy, while professional administrators carry out the technical tasks of government, the comment may well be made that this association of elected amateurs with permanent professionals may mean in practice that the latter make the decisions and the former only provide a façade.

Further questions are raised by the critics of democracy about the adequacy of representative institutions to provide a link between the public and the possessors of political power. Is the right to cast a ballot once every year, or every five years, a meaningful form of political participation, they ask? Even those who work hard within a party organization may find themselves without influence on policy, it is said, since parties are run from behind the scenes by cliques or "bosses" for their own interests. Moreover, it is charged that pressure groups, far from broadening the concern of public figures with community interests, merely focus attention on particular and frequently only local demands, to the detriment of the public at large. Under such circumstances, legislatures are said to be mere conglomerations of warring interests, each seeking to secure the largest slice of public moneys for itself. This becomes the easier, it is pointed out, because most representatives come from constituencies which have little sense of cohesion and, therefore, rarely attempt to influence the votes which are being cast in their name. In any case, it is sometimes questioned whether one man can ever represent the interests and thinking of another, and whether, therefore, the whole notion of representative government is not based on a false premise. To this is added the charge that the information on which the citizen depends both for his judgments on public policy and for making his choice of representatives is apt to be distorted to their own interests by those who control the media of communication: the press, radio, and TV.

Are Its Assumptions Tenable?

The next level of doubts about democracy concerns the capacity of ordinary human beings to make judgments on the complex issues of a modern state. On the one hand, it is pointed out that more and more of the responsibilities of government are technical in character, whether they are concerned with giant roads and bridges or with nuclear power. Moreover, many of the issues that must be decided affect the allocation of resources. But, in addition to questioning the adequacy of average people to make decisions on the affairs and personnel of a government concerned with such matters, there is the nagging uncertainty about whether people can retain that sense of detachment which permits them to separate public needs from their own private and selfish interests, whether they can listen judiciously to both sides of an argument, and whether they will refrain from violence when unpopular programs are put into effect.

How Strong Is Its Appeal?

Finally, in what may well be the deepest of all challenges, it is questioned whether democracy, with its lack of assured program and goals, can answer with anything like the same success as can ideological totalitarianism the need of people for a faith.

This is an age when transcendental religion has lost its hold on many people, and yet it is one in which strains and uncertainties create a particular need for spiritual reinforcement. Fascist or Communist ideologies, with their popular symbols and their certainty about their goals, offer the appeal of a new religion to many who are living in a spiritual vacuum. Even if democracy may be said to satisfy its mature practitioners, there are many who doubt that it can equal the attraction of a totalitarian faith either to those within Western countries who find themselves disadvantaged in the competition for the good things of life, or, more especially, to the still underdeveloped, oftentimes hungry and suffering majority of the world's people, whether in Asia, Africa, or Latin America.

Such an indictment of democracy as has been made brings to the surface some of the commonplaces of political comment; it does little to test their validity. It provides a background, however, against which much of the rest of this book can examine the workings of institutions of mature democracies as well as of developing states and of modern fascist and Communist dictatorships. Politics has the right to be ranked as a science only in so far as its processes are analyzed with the same care as is given to the data of what are commonly called the experimental sciences. This book makes no pretensions to developing a new theory of politics, but it does attempt to examine the workings of different types of political systems and to evaluate their consequences in the light of such information as we now possess. If in so doing it stimulates discussion on the validity of the questions and on the doubts about democracy which have been raised, and on ways in which these questions and doubts might be answered, this, too, will fit into the purpose of the authors.

III

THREE SIGNIFICANT PATTERNS
OF TWENTIETH-CENTURY
GOVERNMENT

Within the dichotomy of democracy and totalitarianism there are, as we have seen, all kinds of subtypes, gradations, and transitions which render the spectrum of political regimes extremely varied and colorful. To deal meaningfully with them, it is necessary to select a few patterns of twentieth-century government that appear especially significant, partly because they are characteristic of the political and governmental structures that prevail in major powers, such as the Soviet Union and China, on the one hand, and the United States and Great Britain, on the other, but partly also because they now constitute the standard forms, as it were, likely to be imitated by new countries as well as by older ones when in the process of changing their institutions. These patterns have emerged partly out of history, partly out of force, and partly out of example.

We concentrate on three of these patterns: one of these characterizes totalitarianism wherever it has arisen in the twentieth century; and two markedly different structures are found among liberal democratic systems. The first is *dictatorship* based on *one-party* rule—with the official or "state" party in turn representing the "movement" and its basic philosophy. This form has been the predominant feature of Communist as well as fascist totalitarianism. Democracy, on the other hand, though exhibiting greater variety, has traditionally operated through either of two distinctive patterns, which have been continued from the eighteenth and nineteenth centuries into the twentieth: the *parliamentary* pattern of Great Britain and the older Commonwealth nations as well as the somewhat different parliamentary systems of west and north European countries; and the *presidential* system of the United States.

The chief difference between the two democratic patterns is that the parliamentary one is based on an interlocking between the legislative and executive branches of government, whereas the presidential system is characterized by the "separation," or more accurately, the independence of these branches, or "powers." As we shall see when we discuss these systems in greater detail, the parliamentary system, in particular, varies in many details, the most important being the distinction between a structure in which the executive more or less dominates the legislature, and one where the legislature dominates the executive. The former relationship is characteristic of the British parliamentary system; the latter was embodied in the traditional French parliamentary structure before the Fifth, or De Gaulle Republic. What characterizes both of these structures and stands in contrast to the separation of powers system is the close interaction—sometimes spoken of as fusion—of the executive and legislative branches of government.

To a large extent, these three systems, one-party dictatorship, parliamentary democracy, and the presidential system, have been adopted by—or imposed upon—many if not most of the countries of the present-day world. It is particularly important, therefore, to understand their basic features.

THE ONE-PARTY DICTATORSHIP

The simplest of all modern political forms is the one-party dictatorship. Its concentration of political authority in the hands of the executive and administration is underpinned by the all-pervasive influence of a highly organized political party which can scarcely be differentiated from the governmental machinery which it operates. Though representative organs are commonly a part of the structure of modern one-party dictatorships, it is not their purpose to provide control, but rather to serve as a sounding board for political pronouncements. Law and the courts do not operate as separate independent entities authorized to decide disputes concerning the operations of other governmental organs, but act to reinforce the norms of behavior laid down by the party leadership and ratified by the executive and administration. This remains true even when these norms are radically changed in response to new objectives. Thus, it is characteristic of one-party dictatorships that all the organs of government—executive, administrative, legislative, and judicial—find their overriding purpose in the objectives of the regime, and that these objectives are formulated by the leaders of the one political party which infiltrates and directs not only political, but also economic, social, and, in principle, even highly personal affairs.

The Soviet Union

The Soviet Union has had by far the longest history of any of the modern one-party dictatorships, and it is possible in its case to identify eras of development. There are three major eras so far, each characterized by the emphasis provided by its dominant figure or figures as well as by the particular conditions and demands of the time.

The first era, under Lenin (and for a short while after his death in the 1920's), was characterized by revolutionary fervor. Although rule was exercised from the top level of the party, the system made some appeal for popular support, or at least for support by, and even a certain feeling of responsibility to, the broader party membership. There followed the culmination of one-man control under Stalin, a regime under which centralized authority backed by brutality, police-terror, and unending purges forced a social and economic revolution in order to create a powerful industrial-military structure.

In the third, post-Stalin era, the Soviet Union still remains a one-party, totalitarian dictatorship, but, compared with the Stalinist period, there have been significant changes, or at least trends toward change. The party, still the dominating institution in the political structure, continues to extend its hold over every aspect of life and society. The early effort, after "de-Stalinization," to substitute collective leadership for personal rule, did not succeed. Under Khrushchev, it led to another personal dictatorship, complete with a modified "cult of personality," which ultimately led to his dethronement and his being turned into an "un-person." But the deposition of Khrushchev constituted the first instance in modern Russian history in which power was turned over "peacefully," through the retirement, not death, of the incumbent and through voting, albeit by a small elite body of the party. At this point it looks as if there is a chance that Khrushchev's successors may be able and willing to exercise control as a collective entity that observes a measure of accountability toward other party bodies.

By the same token, the totalitarian character of the Soviet regime is being gradually alleviated by concessions to initiative, especially in the economic sphere, and by some measure of free, or at least freer, expression and creativity in the realms of science, literature, and the arts. All of this, together with the disappearance of the open terror of the Stalin era, lends the Soviet system increasingly the character of a welfare state, still controlled dictatorially, to be sure, and still with totalitarian features—especially in the realms of opinion-making and education—but one where, as in the case of the fascist-authoritarian dictatorships like that in Spain, the "winds of change"—i.e., the impact of modernization and of the scientific-technological revolution—may in the long run compel the leadership to become less doctrinaire and dogmatic and to go in the direction of more "liberal" approaches.

Other Communist Regimes

Whether such "liberalization" resulting from modernization will turn out to be a "law of development" applicable to *all* Communist countries remains to be seen. In the case of Communist China, which is still in an earlier stage of development, it certainly does not yet apply. Here we have a country that is pressing ahead the socialization of agriculture and village life and the "communization" of all life with a fervor and a ruthlessness exceeding even that of the Soviet Union in the early days of the Five-Year Plan. The wholesale liquidation of "class enemies" and purges has somewhat abated, but one-man dictatorship, complete with personality cult and the use of the entire party machinery for the enforcement and propaganda efforts of the regime, has not. Equally characteristic of the rule in present-day Communist China is the atmosphere of single-minded aims and objectives and of universal mass acclaim, whether genuine or synthetic, which pervades the political, social, and cultural landscape. Mao's success is, perhaps, not so surprising in a nation that for centuries had been beset with internal dissension, the oppression of the people, and a weakness leading to external domination not far short of colonization. In his case, Communism has merely made use of a national awakening which was overdue in any event.

In the East European Communist countries, Communism is as new as in China, yet they much more closely resemble the Soviet Union. This is so not only because of the obvious influence of Soviet developments on the formerly so-called Soviet satellites, but, above all, because these countries—however much they may vary—had not only attained a higher degree of development (apart from cultural achievements) prior to their "communization," but their value systems, traditions, and the general sophistication of the people had more or less made them a part of the West. The introduction of Communism there, while in some way "progressive" in relation to agrarian, industrial, and welfare matters, was thus a retrogression politically and in respect to the cultural and other freedoms their people had been enjoying. Dictatorship in these countries had thus to rely on out-and-out force in a particularly brutal fashion; it became "Stalinist" not only in the sense that the different dictators were the puppets and henchmen of "Big Brother," but in every other sense of the term as well.

On the other hand, with Stalin and Stalinism gone from the Soviet Union, it became relatively easier in Eastern Europe to substitute a more lenient and even "liberal" type of control for that of the Stalinists, whether by quasi-revolutionary change of leadership (as in Poland), by peaceful substitution (as in Bulgaria), by continuation of incumbents now no longer so "absolute" in their control (as in Czechoslovakia and even, albeit minimally, in East Germany), or, strangely, by counterrevolution in which an anti-Communist uprising was put down by the very Communist leader who subsequently liquidated Stalinism (Hungary). Generalization is difficult in this area, for the degree and type of liberalization have varied in time and place during the last decade. Here and there, and always under the looming shadow of a possible "clamping-down" on the part of the regime, people have enjoyed freedom of discussion, cultural experimentation, and even the right to criticism comparable to Western standards. But it is too early to say whether such hopeful beginnings will turn out to have been "waves of the future."

So far it remains true that despite great variation in their use of power and even in the allocation of authority, there has been relatively little variation among these regimes in the political structure itself. To this point, all of them have remained one-party systems based on control from the top level of the party which organizes and dominates the state even where it decentralizes certain functions and allows more leeway to individual and group activities. The key still remains the concentration of power in a single party and its leadership, whose influence permeates society without becoming accountable to any representative institution. This type of regime still provides the most powerful means of centralized and pervasive rule which has as yet been developed.

THE PARLIAMENTARY PATTERN

The pattern of dictatorship is a relatively simple one; the forms of democratic states have endless variety. They revolve around various methods of attempting to secure those purposes of which we spoke when discussing democracy: an effective representation of the electorate; a relation between the organs of representation and the executive which permits leadership and, at the same time, keeps it in constant touch with the elected representatives of the people; and limits on arbitrary use of power by government and its officials. The methods adopted by particular states arise out of historical evolution (particularly obvious in relation to Great Britain); or out of concepts modified by evolution (as in the United States); or out of attempts to correct past inadequacies (as in the Fifth French Republic, with its great strengthening of the executive to avoid the legislative omnipotence and executive instability of the Fourth and even Third French Republics, or as in West Germany); or out of transfer of institutions to former dependent territories (as in the Commonwealth of Nations); or out of a combination of these factors. Within the wide range of democratic forms of government, the most common is the parliamentary pattern, partly because of the influence of British parliamentary experience, but more particularly because of its relative simplicity of organization and apparent ease of operation.

The prime characteristic of the parliamentary form of government is the so-called fusion of the executive and legislature. The executive becomes the governing group not because of a direct vote by the electorate, as in the presidential system, but because it comprises the leaders of one or several parties represented in the legislature who are able to command sufficient support within that body to pass the legislation embodied in their program. In a two-party system, there is no question about which party commands a majority in the legislature; its leaders assume the executive role as soon as an election has made this clear. In a multiparty system, there may well be more difficulty about determining which combination of leaders shall assume the role of the executive. In either case, however, there is an interaction between executive and legislature which keeps them constantly interrelated and dependent on each other, but, at the same time, fulfilling different functions. The executive prepares the program, pushes it through the legislature by personal and direct leadership, and supervises the administration. The members of the legislature consider the details of the program, enact what they decide to approve, criticize or support the executive's and the administration's handling of their responsibilities, and keep alert to the comments of their constituents and to the general reactions of the country to governmental policy. Within the parliamentary system, therefore, there is an intimate association of the executive and legislature, combined with differentiation of function; there is effective government (at least where the parliamentary majority is clear), combined with opportunities—as through the daily question period in the British parliamentary system—for making the executive justify its actions.

Technically, the parliamentary system revolves around the institution of (and procedures for expressing or denying) "confidence" in the executive. Where parliament can force the government (in the sense of the executive) to resign by voting "nonconfidence" in it—or at least compel the executive to dissolve parliament in such a case and appeal to the electorate—the parliamentary system is operating in its classic form. Systems, such as those of present-day France and West Germany, which render such expression of confidence or nonconfidence difficult, if not impossible, are thus of doubtful parliamentary nature; rather, as we suggested earlier, they have aspects of authoritarianism (though one which is limited in time due to legally required periodic elections). Even in Great Britain the expense of fighting elections, the strictness of party disciplines, and general sentiments against too frequent overthrows of a government act against unrestricted use of votes of confidence. In the end, responsiveness to comment and criticism and tolerance of opposition views may elicit "confidence" without the mechanism of the kind of vote on which the survival of an executive technically depends.

The close working together of executive and legislature within the framework of the parliamentary system contrasts with the nonpolitical nature of the judiciary. Judicial independence, which is essential for the maintenance of limitations on political and administrative actions, must be a principle of government in a democratic state; it is reinforced by the fact that judges are chosen from a particular profession (in Great Britain from senior barristers, i.e., those who plead cases in the law courts; in the United States also from the legal profession; and in France, and other European countries, from persons trained for this particular career) and that they have permanent tenure. In Great Britain and France, courts of law do not pass on the constitutionality of legislative acts, but in some parliamentary systems, like those of Canada, Australia, West Germany, and Austria, cases can be taken to a supreme court to determine the constitutionality of legislation in the light of the basic constitutional document. In all democratic systems, however, one court or another can make judgments on the legality of administrative acts by testing them against the statute or ordinance under which the action was taken.

The British Parliamentary System

The British parliamentary system, often looked on as a model of effective yet responsible government, evolved out of two processes operating at different periods of time. The first was one of differentiation of functions which had originally emanated from the person of the monarch, and subsequently was one of limitations on his power. This long process led to the separate jurisdiction of the courts of law, and to documents, notably Magna Carta in 1215, the Petition of Rights in 1628, and the Bill of Rights in 1689—which attempted to prevent the monarch from acting in what was looked on as an arbitrary fashion destructive of customary rights. In the seventeenth century, the House of Commons with its twofold influence—as a grantor of money and as a representative body—assumed the leading role in attempting to limit the monarch, while the execution of Charles I and the deposition of James II made it quite clear that royal power could never again be supreme. The second process began in the mid-eighteenth century, when the king began to select his chief advisers or ministers from persons who had the confidence and support of a majority of the members in the House of Commons. As this principle became established, the reasons for limiting the powers of the Crown disappeared. Thus the British Cabinet, which now wields the powers of the Crown, possesses a wide measure of independent executive authority, as well as the power it secures through its leadership of the legislative body.

This leadership, in contrast to what we may call the older "French" type of parliamentarism (i.e., of the Third and Fourth French Republics), issues not only from the traditional British two-party system, which ordinarily guarantees majority party control in the House of Commons, but also from the established right of the Crown (now exercised by the Prime Minister) to dissolve Parliament. The nonexistence or nonexercise of such a right in the earlier practices of the "French" system, on the other hand, coupled with a poorly disciplined multiparty structure, accounted for the weakness of the executive and the predominance of Parliament in the working of the latter system.

Though the British Cabinet is one of the most powerful executive bodies in the democratic world because of its control of the House of Commons, it nevertheless accepts its responsibility to act for the country as a whole, and not merely as the organ of the majority party. It is kept on the *qui vive* by the constant probing and questioning of the opposition party and by the publicity given to governmental actions and policies by the more responsible portions of the press, and by radio and TV. In a somewhat similar combination of freedom for and restraint on governmental action, the courts in Great Britain do not question the validity of an act of Parliament, but in handling a case in which it is relevant, they proceed from the premise that legislation is meant to be reasonable in intent, that is, to deal fairly and equally with all people. Coupled with the bias toward individual freedom of the common law, out of which have come many of the basic rules of procedure and precedents that mold the workings and judgments of the courts, this "rule of reason" reinforces the civil liberties of which the British are justly proud.

The Parliamentary System in the Commonwealth

The British parliamentary system evolved out of history and through a process extending over centuries. All the more remarkable, therefore, has been the extension of British parliamentary institutions into the countries of the British Empire and thus into the Commonwealth of Nations. Rarely have institutions resembled so closely the parent stock as those of

Canada, Australia, and New Zealand. In each of these countries can be found the system of cabinet responsibility, the parliamentary concentration of power, and what is in essence the two-party system so characteristic of Great Britain.

Yet history and environment have added individual features of major importance in each of these countries. Thus, Canada and Australia are federal systems in which the territorial division of power strains constantly against the unifying pressures of parliamentary rule; moreover, judicial review has played a far greater role in their development than it could in the unitary states of Great Britain and New Zealand, in which the territorial division of functions has no constitutional guarantee. As far as party systems are concerned, Canada follows the American pattern more than it does the British, with both its major parties, the Liberals and Progressive Conservatives, functioning as great holding companies of diverse interests, and only the minority NDP (New Democratic Party) unified by a social program somewhat comparable to that of the Labour Parties of Great Britain, Australia, and New Zealand. When we look at policies, we find that Australia and New Zealand took the lead in early and radical experiments with state ownership and with compulsory arbitration of industrial disputes.

But whatever their divergence from British forms, Canada, Australia, and New Zealand have a basic similarity to Great Britain in political tradition and constitutional attitudes which is far more significant. Underlying this similarity there is not only a common intellectual and political heritage—kept strong by ties of blood constantly refreshed by immigration and by allegiance to a common Crown—but there are also the virtually ideal conditions for democracy possessed by these overseas parts of the Commonwealth. Notable among these conditions are their middle-class structures (so important, as Aristotle pointed out long ago, for the harmonious working of a constitution), widespread economic prosperity, a high degree of social mobility, and a workable balance between industry and agriculture.

Far more remarkable than finding British institutions and parliamentary traditions operating in the older parts of the Commonwealth overseas is to find them also in several of the newer Commonwealth members: India, Malaysia, and Nigeria. Here the rate of literacy is low, the middle class is a small if dominant minority, and poverty is widespread. Yet despite such handicaps, these countries have had considerable success so far in holding democratic elections (using symbols on the ballots, since the overwhelming proportion of voters cannot read), in operating parliamentary institutions, and even in handling that part of the government most difficult for the inexperienced—administration.

Most of the other African states graduating to independence and Commonwealth status—like Ghana, Tanzania (the union of former Tanganyika and the island of Zanzibar) , and Kenya —have turned to one-party structures, but without giving up the pattern of administration and, in the last two countries, the open discussions and the judicial impartiality and independence they inherited from their earlier, British-controlled, experience. But none of the new African and Asian members of the Commonwealth has yet acquired, to any considerable degree, the same overriding loyalty to the interest of the state as to that of the clan, group, or family which insulates administration against corruption. None has the favorable conditions of natural resources and freedom from aggressive outside pressures that the earlier "British" overseas members of the Commonwealth enjoyed. Thus their future remains uncertain, dependent not only on their own efforts but also on the course of international rivalries.

The Parliamentary System in Western Europe

The British pattern is only one facet of what is still the most widespread form of democratic political organization today:

the parliamentary system. Though in general that system is characterized by the dependence of the executive on the confidence of the legislature, there can be wide differences in executive-legislative relations. In the British form of parliamentary government, the executive dominates the legislature, partly because, with rare exceptions, it is not parliament but the people through their votes who, in practice, choose the executive. In a sense, therefore, the legislature in British countries acts like an electoral college, as far as the creation of cabinets is concerned, though, unlike other electoral colleges, it continues in existence, discussing, criticizing, and passing upon the policies of the government. In the earlier French system, on the other hand, the legislature dominated the executive because it had created it and also because it could not be dissolved by it. A net result of these and other differences is that while Great Britain has a strong, stable cabinet, France used to have a weak, unstable one.

France: What we have called the traditional and earlier French system is that of the Third and of the Fourth Republic, which came into being at the end of World War II and ended in 1958. The Third, and even more so the Fourth Republic, provided obvious examples of the problems that arise when a too-powerful legislature, torn by a multiparty system (in which, after World War II, both the extreme left—the Communists—and from time to time also the extreme right were antidemocratic), results in an unstable executive incapable of providing consistent and effective leadership. The Constitution of the Fifth French Republic is designed to correct this imbalance and has done so to such a degree that France, since 1958, has been governed by what is less a parliamentary regime than a mixture of authoritarianism and technocracy, with technical experts directing administration under the general supervision of the Cabinet (of which they are important members) and of the President, General Charles de Gaulle. This system tending toward the authoritarian has been taken over completely, and indeed to a still fuller degree—because they have turned their countries into single constituencies in which the winning party takes all the seats—by the former French-controlled African territories from Guinea to Congo (Brazzaville).

Under the Fifth French Republic, no Cabinet member may also be a member of the National Assembly, as all members were in the Fourth French Republic, though he can appear before that body to direct discussions and explain policy. The Cabinet now has specific independent powers it did not possess before, while the Assembly, far from being omnipotent, is almost impotent, being limited in its periods of meeting and restricted in debate. The President is no longer selected by the votes of the National Assembly and Senate meeting jointly, as under the Fourth French Republic (on one occasion, the crippling force of party divisions resulted in more than one hundred ballots). Under the original Gaullist Constitution, the President was chosen by elected local office holders throughout the country. However, by an amendment of 1962, itself adopted under procedures of doubtful constitutionality, the President will be selected by direct popular election—a plebiscitarian device known to, and distrusted by, Frenchmen ever since first used by the two Napoleons. This process is meant to bestow on future presidents the kind of prestige De Gaulle possesses because of his own mystique. The President in the Fifth French Republic already possesses substantial reserve powers under which he can act if the Cabinet should ever cease to provide effective executive control, but beyond this De Gaulle has kept under his own personal direction substantial areas, including foreign policy, that in the British parliamentary system would be controlled by the Cabinet. Thus under De Gaulle, the Fifth French Republic has a strong presidential cast, and it might even be said that his regime has something of the character of a monarchy of the days when the king ruled and reigned.

West Germany: To some degree, therefore, the Gaullist Fifth Republic fits into a kind of prototype of regimes in-between parliamentarism and new-style authoritarianism. Seeing what has emerged in West Germany since World War II, it is difficult to deny a similar trend toward such a form. In West Germany, another of the remarkable "grand old men" who in the postwar period determined the fate of some nations, had a dominant influence in providing effective leadership within what had been conceived of as basically a parliamentary type of government. To be sure, to compare the system that grew under Chancellor Konrad Adenauer's fourteen-year rule with the at least half-authoritarian structure of the French Fifth Republic would not be entirely appropriate. But the Bonn system contains features that do cast some doubt on the degree of genuine parliamentary democracy in West Germany.

It is clear that the system was intended to provide Germans with a genuine parliamentary pattern of government. But the pre-Nazi Weimar system, whose extreme parliamentarianism had resulted in an instability comparable to that of the Third French Republic, strongly influenced the drafters of the Bonn Constitution. Consequently, they devised built-in guarantees of executive stability, such as the so-called constructive vote of nonconfidence, which makes it necessary for a party or parties desiring to overthrow the incumbent Chancellor to present a candidate backed by a new majority before the incumbent can be forced to resign.

Since in other respects the Federal Assembly constitutionally enjoys the customary rights and privileges of a parliament in a full-fledged parliamentary democracy, this stipulation might not have been so important had not other factors combined to strengthen the executive at the expense of the powers and prestige of parliament. Under any circumstances, a country like Germany, not accustomed in the past to the habits of government by discussion and consent, would have had a hard time growing into such ways of political life. As it happened, the forceful personality of Adenauer, the prototype of the German statesman interested in *having things done* rather than in *how* they were done, presided over the reconstruction of West Germany after the Nazi breakdown and defeat. By good luck and management, this reconstruction period proved to be one of unexcelled economic prosperity as well as unequalled rise to eminence in the foreign field, thereby greatly contributing to the reputation of his government. To Germans, habitually looking to the expert leader in political, executive, and administrative affairs to handle matters without much participation and initiative on their part, Adenauer's regime provided a chance to see efficiency combined with representative government. But the latter was bound to suffer. Adenauer lost no time in establishing the principle that ministers, far from being coresponsible members of the Cabinet and separately responsible to Parliament, were his own aides exclusively. In addition, many fields, such as foreign affairs, were for long periods eliminated from parliamentary purview, and the prestige and standing of the Bundestag therefore declined in public esteem.

Another trend, one toward a "one-and-a-half party" system rather than a two-party system, has contributed to this process. Since the Christian Democrats have been in office since the inception of the Bonn regime, the other major party, the Social Democrats, has been left in ineffectual and frustrated opposition, an opposition which has found little outlet through debate and criticism in Parliament or elsewhere. In neither economic nor foreign affairs have they developed policy alternatives fused into an attractive program, and thus there has been the danger that the dominant party might perpetuate its control with the ensuing danger of petrified elites and self-serving interests. However, a more recent development may yet give a chance to the two-party system and party alternation in office, namely, the weakness in leadership displayed by Ludwig Erhard, Adenauer's successor to the Chancellorship, in domestic as well as foreign affairs. This factor may provide the Social Democrats with a chance to make inroads into the nonlabor part of the electorate which would make them the majority party. German democracy might then function on the same basis as does liberal democracy in other two-party systems, such as those of the United States and Canada and, increasingly, that of Great Britain, namely by two moderate parties both appealing to a broad spectrum of the electorate.

Italy: There remains only one other major country in continental Europe—Italy—where the traditional parliamentary system still holds sway. The numerous falls and crises of government which it has suffered since the end of the war remind one of the Third and Fourth French Republics as well as of its own prefascist history. There was a period, from the fifties into the early sixties, when the future of the parliamentary system in Italy seemed particularly endangered because of the radicalism and combined strength of the parties of the right (neo-Fascists and Monarchists) and, even more particularly, of the left (Communists and Nenni Socialists), which were in permanent opposition to the prevailing system as such. With the more recent policy of the "opening to the left," under which the Nenni Socialists were split away from their alignment with the Communists and were induced to join the government coalition, more stability seems to have been achieved. The Christian Democrats are apparently no longer dependent on the uncertain backing of small groups, though unfortunately for their power position, the Christian Democrats themselves have revealed an increasing tendency to split into warring factions, finding it ever more difficult to unite on common policies. Thus the future of parliamentary democracy in Italy remains in doubt, as it does in Greece, which in this respect resembles Italy.

On the other hand, as we survey other European parliamentary systems, we find that most of them are much more stable and function better than do the Italian and Greek systems.

The Netherlands and Scandinavia: In the Netherlands, Sweden, and Norway, the executive is weaker than in Great Britain, but much more stable than in France's Fourth Republic. In the Netherlands, for example, the multiparty system, as was true in France, throws the choice of the ministry into the chamber; occasionally, there are cabinet crises lasting several months before a ministry is formed. But once chosen, the cabinet, and even more the Prime Minister, tend to retain office for relatively long periods of time. This can partly be explained by two characteristics of these parliamentary systems: Cabinet and legislature are separated more from each other than in Great Britain or West Germany, yet that there is far more give-and-take between the two in hammering out the legislative program.

These West European countries thus have a very different view than do the British of the relation between the executive and the legislature. The executive in the Scandinavian countries and in the Netherlands tends both to bargain more and to be more adjustable. To have the legislature reject an important part of the Cabinet's program is not looked on as a major defeat, as it would be in Great Britain. On the contrary, when the executive proposes a project, it anticipates not only that this project will be carefully considered in the legislature, as is true in Great Britain, but possibly also modified. It accepts this situation. Thus, these countries tread a middle way between the possible "cabinet dictatorship" of the British parliamentary system (which, in Britain itself, is avoided by the self-restraint of the Cabinet), and the executive instability of the Fourth French Republic. The result is a system marked by compromise and a genuine executive-legislative partnership in the making of law.

Switzerland: The relation between parliament and executive in Switzerland deviates from the usual parliamentary pattern to such an extent that some students of comparative government consider the "Swiss system" to be a third type, to be distinguished from either the normal parliamentary or the presidential system. Once elected by parliament, the federal councilors who make up the seven-member Swiss executive never resign over any issue of policy which divides them, individually or as a body, from a parliamentary majority. They continue to preside over their departments, following the instructions of Parliament. Since, furthermore, Parliament cannot be dissolved under the Swiss system, the political interplay between legislature and executive which is characteristic of other parliamentary systems, and which may lead to resignations, dissolutions, and new elections in the wake of votes of nonconfidence, does not exist in Switzerland. Thus the Swiss executive might be considered a top-level bureaucracy rather than a policy-making, issue-resolving separate "power." Issues are resolved either in parliament or by popular vote (initiative and referendum), a typical Swiss institution. Since Switzerland's permanent neutrality prejudges most of its foreign-policy problems, and many domestic problems are handled on the cantonal level, issues tend, however, to be less serious and numerous than in other West European democracies.

The bureaucratic nature of the Swiss executive is further apparent from the usually long tenure of individual councilors, extending frequently over many parliamentary terms. These re-elections are possible because—in another deviation from the usual parliamentary pattern—the Federal Council comprises representatives of all the major parties regardless of

election results, although not on a proportionate basis. Moreover, the body functions as a truly collegiate group. There is
nobody who might be compared to a prime minister, not even
as "first among equals." This reflects the fact that the Swiss
executive does not provide political leadership. In a way,
Switzerland has perhaps the truest "parliamentary" system of
all, since Parliament is in charge of all important decisions and
the executive is a mere committee of that body, without political ambitions of its own. There, the system has been highly
successful in combining democratic responsibility and representation with stability of government. But it is questionable
whether it could function equally well in larger and more
divided nations lacking the broad constitutional and general
consensus with which the closely knit Swiss community is
blessed.

Austria: A still different and even stranger kind of system
has developed in postwar Austria. There, in striking contrast
to Switzerland, Parliament has been emasculated both in its
role as legislature and as supervisor of the executive by virtue
of the fact that the two major parties, the Socialists and the
People's Party (which in postwar elections have always been
almost equal in strength) work together in a government coalition that leaves little room for effective opposition. The resulting executive "cartel" functions on the basis of an initial
compact which, clearly and in detail, outlines agreed-upon policies and which, therefore, are not opposed by either of the two
parties in the Cabinet or Parliament. The machinery of administration, in turn, is divided among the two parties on the basis
of "parity," so that for each position assigned to one there is an
equivalent office for the other. Jokingly it has been asked
whether, in case one tenor at the Vienna State Opera happens
to be from the People's Party, there must be another with Socialist affiliation. This division of state offices and the absence

of effective opposition have their obvious shortcomings; but the system is defended by Austrians as a far lesser evil than the possible alternative, which existed in the post-World War I period, in which social classes and their party representatives were so deeply divided that they ultimately clashed in a civil war in 1934. While the earlier Austrian experience terminated in dictatorship, the present one at least permits the functioning of a system, pseudo-parliamentary though it may be, that seems to guarantee the peaceful coexistence of the two parties without major infractions of individual or group rights and liberties. In addition, the greater moderation of both major parties in the postwar period has been a factor in making this joint control workable.

What is apparent from such a survey is that the parliamentary system is infinitely flexible in adapting to local situations and traditions. By facilitating close executive-legislative relations, this system makes it easy to combine leadership with representative institutions. Familiarity with the parliamentary form may have been an important reason why former colonies of Great Britain adopted it on achieving their independence, but it is also attractive because of its easy adaptability to their needs. It is also adaptable to the republican institutions and presidential power assumed in most former British territories in Africa and Asia. Those formerly under France have adopted a presidential, quasi-parliamentary form modeled on that of De Gaulle's France rather than on the American form of presidential system, which, in an earlier generation, was adopted by the newly independent states of Latin America and by Liberia.

THE PRESIDENTIAL PATTERN

The presidential pattern of government is the other great type of representative democracy. Its distinctive feature, in contrast to parliamentary government, is that the chief executive holds office whether or not he is supported by the majority of the legislature. As the 1956 American election demonstrated, the voters may even elect a Republican President at the same moment that they send a Democratic majority to both chambers. These circumstances furnish an extreme example of the constant give-and-take between executive and legislature that characterizes Continental parliamentary systems like those of Norway and the Netherlands. Even when the American President's party dominates the legislature, the President has less assurance of control over the passage of laws than even a weak British Prime Minister. Yet at the same time, there are great resources at the disposal of an American President. He is the leader of his party, he controls the administration, and he can appeal directly to the people to support his program. Underwriting these sources of power is his guaranteed possession of office for four years, twice the term of office of the lower house.

As with the British parliamentary system, the characteristic features of the American Presidential system are founded in history. It is important to remember that the American Constitution was drafted not in 1776, at the moment of proclaiming independence from Great Britain, when reaction against executive power was at its height, but in 1787, more than a decade later, when the balance had swung sharply, and many of the framers of the Constitution thought dangerously, in favor of powerful legislatures within the states which were enacting radical economic measures in response to the pressures of popular majorities. The Constitution was thus designed to erect a strong national government able to curb the excesses of the states in the interests of financial stability, and within that national government to establish effective checks on the power of the lower house, the most direct agent of the people.

Hence it provided for the establishment of a strong second chamber, the Senate, whose members were originally appointed by state legislatures, and who are still elected for six-year terms, in contrast to the two-year terms of representatives in the lower house. Hence, too, it safeguarded the independence of the chief executive, the President, whose selection through an electoral college was intended to make him only indirectly responsible to the people and whose four-year term completes the pattern of staggered elections. The President was given the power to veto laws, to nominate officials, and to command the army. Moreover, although his veto of laws can be overridden by a two-thirds majority of the members of both the Senate and the House of Representatives, the Constitution provided for the so-called "pocket veto," which makes it impossible to override a Presidential veto of measures passed at the end of a Congressional session.

Lastly, to complete the pattern of checks and balances within the national government, there is the strong position of the Federal judiciary (whose members are appointed for life by the President with the consent of the Senate) and, in particular, of the Supreme Court. Whether the framers of the Constitution intended the Supreme Court to have the power of judicial review is still disputed, but in practice it has exercised that power since Chief Justice John Marshall claimed it in *Marbury* v. *Madison* in 1803. His decision, in 1819, in *Mc-Culloch* v. *Maryland* opened the way to a continuous broadening of the powers and functions of the national government by asserting that the Constitution provides implied as well as explicitly delegated powers. This means that Congress may choose whatever means it considers appropriate for carrying out its legitimate purposes, as long as these means are not specifically prohibited. No less significant, the judgment reaffirmed the precedent that it is the Supreme Court which determines whether or not an act of Congress is constitutional, i.e., has binding force because it is enacted within its legally possessed powers.

Not only is the American Presidential system characterized

by the *functional* division of national power, maintained by the checks and balances among the three, specifically separated, branches—the executive, legislature, and judiciary—but also by the *territorial* division of power between the Federal Government and those of the states. It would have been impossible to establish a national government in 1787 without leaving a considerable amount of power in the hands of the state units, which had been exercising independent authority since the Declaration of Independence. Federalism was also looked on as a further application of the theory of checks and balances by which rash acts on the part of individual states or the national government could be restrained.

Some of the obviously restrictive features of the original Constitution have been changed by formal amendment. Since 1913, Senators have been elected directly by the voters of their states; the franchise has been broadened, and constitutional provisions forbid discrimination on grounds of sex or race (though the country still faces serious problems in preventing the latter). But by far the greatest changes have come through what may be called the unwritten constitution which has grown up alongside the formal Constitution. Party activities, nominating conventions, the President's Cabinet, all these are part of the unwritten constitution, which has arisen out of usage, judicial decisions, and legislation. The popular control that keeps both executive and legislature in the national and state spheres responsive to public pressure is almost solely the result of an evolution that has gone on both inside and outside the formal Constitution.

Despite this evolution and its basic responsiveness to popular sentiment, built-in restraints and the balance of powers remain the characteristics of the American Presidential system. While the machinery of government can act swiftly in response to a national emergency such as posed by war or depression, the constitutional provisions for dividing authority—separation of powers, bicameralism (of two more or less equally powerful chambers), and judicial review—combine to prevent or impede major changes in policy until public pressures have built up on a broad scale. Whereas the parliamentary system responds quickly to popular majorities, the American Presidential system reinforces the position of powerful and organized minorities, e.g., of Middle Western farm interests and of white Southerners through their disproportionately high representation (in proportion to population) in the Senate and on committees of the House of Representatives and Senate concerned with issues in which they have particular interest.

It is at the committee level that the power structure within Congress has so much effect. In contrast to the Cabinet's constant control of legislation and the budget in the British parliamentary system, specialized committees of Congress determine the fate not only of legislation proposed by their own members, but also of proposals for legislative and budgetary measures emanating from the chief executive. Woodrow Wilson once characterized the American system as "a government by the chairmen of the standing committees of Congress." Under the seniority rule, committee chairmen get to be chairmen because they have been on a committee longer than any other member of the party holding a majority in that chamber. This provides a strong advantage to those states or districts which re-elect their representatives over and over again: among the Republicans, this advantage accrues to some of the northern areas; among the Democrats, to the South. Since party cohesion and discipline is far less strong in Congress than in the great majority of parliamentary systems, these provisions (which are based on convention and are not necessarily a part of the congressional-presidential system) reinforce the power position of certain local, sectional, or economic interests.

Those who believe strongly in majority rule and want a system which will smoothly and swiftly translate majority wishes into legislation will favor the parliamentary system over the presidential. Those who are concerned about the dangers of impulsive popular pressures and about the protection of vested groups and interests may well favor the presidential-congressional, or separation-of-powers, system. It is obvious that each has its own particular problems and requires a particular type of restraint and experience to operate in such a fashion as to secure effective results in needed legislation without degenerating into irresponsible majority rule.

Like the British parliamentary system of government, the American Presidential system has provided a model for the government of many states. As noted above, the republics of Latin America have copied, to a greater or lesser extent, the structure devised by the American Constitution. Except in rare instances, this has been done of their own accord and not through any American tutelage comparable to the British and French experiments in developing colonies toward self-government through the progressive handing-over of responsibility for operating their institutions. For better or, in some cases, for worse, Latin American countries and (though less so now) Liberia have had to struggle largely unaided to make their American-type institutions operate. In a considerable number of situations, as we will see, the results bear little resemblance to the parent model. This is sometimes true also in regard to those newer countries which have adopted the parliamentary system or some variant of it. Thus we may well ask: How deep does Western influence go among the developing countries of Latin America, Africa, the Middle East, and Asia?

How Deep Does Western Influence Go?

Taking into account the degree of imitation of the governmental forms of Great Britain, France, the United States, and the Soviet Union, we might be tempted to say that the ideas of

Locke and Harrington, Montesquieu and Rousseau, Bentham and Mill, and Hegel and Marx have by and large been the determinants of the modern world. But to what degree has this been more than a surface influence? Is it not possible that the few centuries in which these ideas and their attendant institutions have flourished constitute, at least for the non-Western world, what an Indian author has called the "Vasco da Gama age"? In other words, has this perhaps been merely a transitory period of superficial Western influence over a non-Western world again shaping its own destinies? Or, to ask a different question: Has the Western influence in fact been strong enough to establish Western democratic ways in countries whose background and conditions of life are so essentially dissimilar to those of the middle-class democracies of the United States, Great Britain, Canada, Australia, and New Zealand?

If we study Latin-American life, for instance, we are struck by the frequent discrepancy between the constitutional framework (and its underlying ideological assumptions) and the political reality. The Latin-American mind—that is, the mind of its intellectuals—steeped as it is in Anglo-American or, more often, Continental-European traditions, tends to be legalistic; it loves to indulge in the niceties of formal constitutional arguments and interpretations without great regard as to whether they are meaningful. Actually, of course, one must distinguish between Latin American states for which such a generalization is valid and those for which it is not. Advanced nations like Chile or Uruguay have been able to make institutions and constitutions of a Western type much more meaningful than others in South America, like Peru or Bolivia, for instance, where a majority of the population, in many cases Indians, still live under the primitive conditions of the age of discoveries; or where a one-crop or one-resource economy concentrates wealth in a tiny (formerly usually foreign, now mixed foreign-indigenous) upper class. In countries like Chile and Uruguay, there exists a basis for political stability and even democracy. In the less advanced nations of Latin America, it is hardly surprising to find that political power tends to be concentrated in the hands of one man (the *caudillo*) or of a small group, commonly of military men (*junta*). Thus in the curious and extreme instance of the Dominican Republic, there was for decades a concentration of almost all the national wealth in the *caudillo's* own hands, for Trujillo, together with members of his family, owned most of the enterprises (which remained tax-exempt), and even a large part of the landed property of "his" country. In certain other instances, it is among a small number of educated and Europeanized families that political (together with economic and social) control has circulated.

Thus we see that constitutions and similar organizational rules can mean little; in some cases they may be merely convenient tools for attaining or maintaining power. In Honduras, for instance—to give an example of a situation which is not unique—the constitution provides that a president must stand for re-election after a certain period of office; if no candidate receives 51 per cent of the vote, congress is then empowered to elect the president by a two-thirds majority of the legal membership. But we soon discover that the incumbent usually knows how to get 51 per cent of the vote; if he has not received it, he may see to it that congress has no quorum, in which case the constitutional order is considered "broken" and the incumbent continues in power. Or, as often happens, a constitution which thus limits a president's term or his re-eligibility is simply "amended" (or replaced with a new one) so as to eliminate the obnoxious provision. Constitutions thus are liable to frequent and rapid change, often following upon a *Putsch*. Indeed, and paradoxically, it has been said that something is wrong with political life in a Latin American republic if there are no violent changes once in a while; for long-enduring quiet under one and the same constitution frequently indicates a protracted dictatorship, while a breach of the constitutional order may indicate democratic stirrings. More often, sadly, it merely indicates a change in top-level control.

The more advanced Latin American countries rarely have this kind of *caudillo* regime. But even here, most of them enjoy neither the long tradition of liberal-democratic and constitutional ideas nor the broad middle class which promoted such ideas in the older democracies. As a consequence, their institutions are less stable than those of more mature democracies. Thus in a country like Brazil, democracy may alternate with dictatorship or, as happened in 1956, an army coup to forestall another antidemocratic coup may be required in order to enable the duly elected president to assume office. The progress to a stable constitutional order is thus frequently a halting one.

The importance of economic equality and lack of racial cleavage for the development of democratic constitutionalism is exemplified by the vivid contrast in Central America between democratic Costa Rica and its neighbors. The former has a broad and fairly equal distribution of land among an almost uniformly white population, whereas in the latter there are small, feudal elites of Spanish origin which own most of the wealth and control the predominant Indian or mixed population both economically and politically. The instability of these countries contrasts sharply with the continuity of democratic rule in Costa Rica. Still more striking, the efforts to restore constitutionalism after protracted periods of *caudillo* rule or civil war and to forestall new coups on the part of opposition parties has led Colombia to adopt a unique "system of alternation," in which, through solemn agreement between the two major parties, control alternates successively, so that it is exercised first by the one and then by the other. Even so, this system has been threatened with the danger of coups by formerly powerful political chieftains.

It is obvious that such instability, or even reactionism, under conditions of the "rising expectations" of the masses, of population increases and of beginning modernization and growing urbanization, provides great temptation and many opportunities for radical-revolutionary movements. These are now stimulated by the Castro revolution and propaganda, which is the more potent since it comes from one of the members of the Latin American group. Castroite or similar versions of Communist-led proletarian movements have thus made their appearance especially among peons or impoverished farmers (as in Northern Brazil). Indeed, nowhere in the world today do conditions seem more favorable for radical political change, and, possibly, revolutionary overthrow of established government, than in some of the Latin American countries. The future of democracy there seems to depend less on institutional devices and governmental procedures than on the rapid improvement of living conditions of all of society rather than merely of a tiny upper group. Only thus can programs for modernization, such as those of the Alliance for Progress, succeed.

In such conditions, formal democracy may even have to wait until countries have gone through a preliminary stage of what may be called an "educational" dictatorship which provides for rapid modernization and thus can lay the basis for subsequent, more democratic developments. Outside the Latin American orbit, Turkey, in which Kemal Ataturk Westernized his nation by means of a dictatorship operating through a one-party system, provides an outstanding example of this. It is questionable, in fact, whether without his dictatorship it would have been possible to transform Turkey from a typically Oriental, Islamic, traditionalist country into a modern nation—considering that this involved not only drastic political and economic change, but the destruction of deeply rooted customs (the abolition of the harem, the veil, the fez, and the caliphate;

and the introduction of the Western alphabet, script, and calendar, for example). As the Turkish experience seemed to show, gradual democratization may indeed follow such a transformation, though the re-establishment of army rule in 1960 and subsequent instability of government would suggest that the foundation was less firmly established than had been hoped.

On the other hand, the old feudal interests or those of foreign capital may turn to their own purposes apparently democratic institutions, in particular parliaments which are controlled or have been bought by them. This was the situation in Egypt before its national revolution in 1953. It is still the case in Iran, where the feudal landowning interests dominate parliament, while the ruler himself, the Shah, has emerged as the leader of a movement to reshape the socioeconomic structure of the nation through agrarian reform. More often, however, the movement toward change comes from below and, in the name of economic and social reform (and often with an anti-Western or anti-"Yankee" slant), establishes a "Kemalist" type of regime, such as the Estenssoro rule in Bolivia, or the various Mexican regimes since that country's national revolution in 1917.

If economic, social, and cultural reforms lead toward eventual political democratization, then authoritarianism or even dictatorship may turn out to have been a blessing in disguise. But it is also true that the procedures used during the educational phase may of themselves create that corruption and cynicism which are so dangerous to genuine democracy. This applies especially to voting. Thus, in the 1954 elections to the Iranian Majlis (parliament), bands of the Shah's supporters saw to it that his candidates won out over all others. As newspapers reported, "admiring police and soldiers frequently helped Shaban [the Shah's group] beat victims before arresting them." One voter, before leaving the polling place, was reported to have salaamed three times in the direction of the ballot box;

asked why he had done so, he replied: "I am merely making my obeisance to the magic box. When one drops a ballot in for Mohammed [the ousted Premier Mossadegh], lo, when the box is opened, it is transformed into a vote for Fazdollah [the Shah's man]."*

THE EXTENT OF DIVERSITY

From what has been said so far, it is clear that in addition to similar patterns among governmental systems there is also a colorful (and sometimes dismaying) diversity, one which is constantly increasing as more and more countries acquire their independence. Fifty years ago, there were fewer than fifty sovereign nations; today there are more than one hundred, with still more to come. Some of these countries are still in the primitive stage of civilization, with nomadic forms of life and feudal, absolutistic institutions. Even within one region such as the Middle East, countries of this type, like Saudi Arabia and Yemen, lie close to advanced countries like Lebanon, with its sophisticated, commercial population, and Israel, with its high degree of organization in every aspect of life. Moreover, the degree of control may range all the way from government regulation and organization of almost everything to a bare minimum of government and administration in the operational sense. For example, in 1951, organized government in Syria temporarily ceased to function: the cabinet had resigned and ceased to operate, and government officials had gone on strike. But nothing catastrophic, in fact nothing whatsoever, happened. Life went on as before, unaffected by this idyllic interlude of anarchy. *The New York Times* reported on August 6, 1951:

> Few people noticed that the entire administrative system of the Republic, together with the Government, had been out of action. What the situation amounted to was a demonstration of how

* *The New York Times,* March 11, 12, 1954.

superficial in many ways modern state institutions are in this part of the world. The age-old society that had carried on through wars and catastrophes simply went along as usual.

But while this was possible in a region where at that time feudalism still provided the bulk of the people with known and accepted rules of behavior, such a condition would, of course, create chaos in an industrial society based on far-reaching division of labor.

Finally, to mention one further diversity, there are countries which are formally independent but which only function economically, as well as politically and administratively, with the aid of foreign experts who, as advisers or employees of the indigenous government, actually run the country. For instance, when Lybia was established under United Nations auspices in 1951 as an independent country of federal and monarchical structure, only a handful of its citizens had the training to fill any position in government and administration, while in the 1960's, the tragic case of the Congo re-emphasized the gap between need and human resources, between formal independence and actual viability. Under such circumstances, it may make little difference, at least initially, whether the form of government is democratic or authoritarian, monarchical or republican, unitary or federal.

The Trend Toward Uniformity

But despite all this, we should not exaggerate the factor of diversity. Behind the impression of great variety is a trend toward greater uniformity. Even though the impact of Western ideas and institutions has not (or not yet) been able to "modernize" (in Western terms) the actual political structure and life of many countries which have adopted an outwardly Western constitution or similar façade, most of them are beginning to modernize their economic structure, in particular to industrialize themselves in order to attain higher standards of living.

This is part of that scientific-technological revolution, with its attendant rapid and accelerating change in all fields of life which, as we emphasized at the beginning, forms the perhaps overarching, most decisive new feature of the twentieth-century world. In the face of this all-important development we may even question whether the great diversity of political patterns and systems, including that of the polar opposites—totalitarianism and democracy—will in the future be as significant as the increasing underlying similarity of living conditions and "ways of life." Indeed, there are those who claim to discern a growing likeness of such conditions and even attitudes, at least among the "common people" of such political opposites as the United States and the Soviet Union, with the people in the United States getting used to more and more planning of their lives by big government and other "big" organizations and institutions, while the people in the most modernized Communist countries (comprising not only the Soviet Union but also such former "satellites" as Czechoslovakia and Poland), though accustomed to such inclusion in the big apparatus, are being given some "liberal" discretion in a number of areas. The fact that former Soviet Premier Khrushchev and former American Vice-President Nixon shared their admiration for an American model kitchen exhibited in Moscow may yet prove symptomatic of future developments.

In the face of this trend toward modernization, the more traditionalist types of government, such as feudal and absolutist monarchies, inevitably decline. Traditionalism, even of the tribal type, is bound to give way when the "revolution of rising expectations," with its demands for the better life promised by scientific thought and industrial technology, penetrates areas in which fatalism had hitherto made people shun ideas of change and transformation. Once the expectation of rapid change is aroused, it cannot be stopped by inherited political institutions. Nothing, perhaps, distinguishes our age more sharply from preceding ages than the rate at which change is taking place. While populations are increasing at a fantastic rate and the number of independent countries is constantly growing, there is at the same time an ever-increasing interdependence among nations, arising out of mutual exploitation of resources, growing specialization of functions and, perhaps above all, the awareness that all countries, even the most powerful, are at the mercy of the appalling destructiveness of atomic and hydrogen weapons.

While it is obvious that traditional and feudal forms of government will steadily be overborne by economic change, and particularly by industrialism, it is far from certain that this development will lead these countries toward more democratic forms of government. There was a time when it was taken for granted that an advanced industrial country would be a democracy, but the interwar and postwar periods have undermined this belief. Totalitarianism, fascist or Communist, made deep inroads into regions where democracy seemed firmly established, or at least seemed to have a chance.

This means that the trend toward uniformity, which is particularly strong in the field of technology and, consequently, in areas of industrial and general organization of life, economy, and society, has not, or not yet, been so strong in the area of political systems and governmental structures. There, the trend is not toward a single model or blueprint for political organization; rather it is still toward either of the two opposing models which we have distinguished—the democratic or the dictatorial—or toward one or the other of those less easily characterized middle forms which lean toward one or the other. It is time, therefore, now to examine with some care the framework of limited government, the channels of political action, the role of executives, administration, and pressure groups, and the impact of belief systems and of international relations before we can come to more general conclusions about the prospects of democracy in an increasingly integrating and yet deeply divided world.

IV

THE FRAMEWORK OF LIMITED GOVERNMENT

ORIGINS AND FUNCTIONS OF CONSTITUTIONS

Constitutions define, and thereby limit, public power. The distinctive characteristics of a totalitarian dictatorship, as we have indicated above, are the facts that the power exercised by its governing group is unlimited and unrestrained, and that in principle the authority of the regime extends into every aspect of the life of the individual—religious, cultural, economic, and social. In contrast, the exercise of political power in a liberal democracy is limited by a constitutional framework which protects certain areas of personal and group life from governmental interference and provides that governmental powers shall be exercised in accordance with known procedures. The distinction between the two forms of government is basically, therefore, that between limited and unlimited government.

Genuine constitutions determining these limitations can exist therefore only in nontotalitarian countries. Formal appearances notwithstanding, totalitarian regimes do not have them. At best, such regimes may enjoy merely a self-limitation on the part of the ruling group. And in any case, whatever rules exist are forever provisional, changeable, revocable; they do not have the nature of generality, reliability, and thus calculability which the rules of law elsewhere possess. Genuine constitutionalism is likewise absent when constitutions are forever made and remade, changed and abolished, so as to fit the political needs of the respective power-holders, as is all too often true in Latin American countries.

There were times, in premodern ages, when constitutional rules delimiting the power of rulers were likewise absent. Yet such rule, even when it was presumed to be by divine right, was not totalitarian, since it was generally felt that rulers operated under a religious, moral, or natural law that was supposed to bind ruler and ruled alike. Thus the problem of political theory and practice was pre-eminently a personal one: how to educate the prince, for instance, so that he would govern for the common good. With the rise of the modern territorial state, however, and its impersonal and bureaucratic ordering of many spheres, government became too complicated to depend solely on the personal equation. Reliance was then put on the formulation and formalization of rules.

This does not imply that a constitution is always a written document which was adopted at a particular moment in history as a comprehensive regulation of governmental life. The British Constitution developed gradually, and largely in the form of custom. Yet what made the result of this process a constitution in the modern sense of the word was the fact that it not only defined but *limited* the power of the governing agencies. In the absence of this limiting function, the collections of rules and customs which during this same period—the later Middle Ages and early modern times—defined the arrangements of other political units did not form constitutions in this same sense.

Modern written constitutions arose in the past either from "pact" or from "compact." They arose from *pact* where, as in Continental Europe, they resulted from the contest between popular movements and royal absolutism over a share in political power. Thus, in the typical case of the Continental "constitutional monarch" of the nineteenth century, a written constitution would formalize a compromise between the crown and the people, or the crown and the estates, under which the previously unlimited power of the crown was now formally restrained. They arose from *compact* where, as in the United States, Canada, and Australia, nations were established under commonly agreed-upon rules, the "higher law" under which the people now vowed to live.

Even to this day, most constitutions reflect one or the other of these origins. In the first case, that of pact, the chief function of a constitution is likely to be the delimitation of the spheres of social classes, economic groups, castes, or other groups. In the case of compact, the chief importance of the constitution is as the symbol of unity, since it integrated the nation into one political unit. The delimitation of the spheres of power in this latter type of situation is between institutions which perform distinctive tasks—e.g., legislative and judicial—rather than between historically entrenched groups. The delimitation may also be between territorial divisions and the nation—i.e., federalism—but this rests likewise on the original and basic agreement of the whole people or their original constituent units on how they are to be governed.

Sometimes constitutions having their origin in pact turn into compact, as in the case of Great Britain, where the original Constitution (in this case, a mixture of written and unwritten but accepted rules) first determined the partition of power between the King and nobles, and then between Crown and Parliament, but finally came to reflect the consensus under which the British people rule themselves. In this case, the sense for constitutionalism—i.e., abiding by rules that determine the allocations and use of political power—is joined to the sense of national unity. On the other hand, where, as in Germany, the basis for the original pact has disappeared and later constitutions have failed to attain the symbolic character of the Constitution in the United States, constitutionalism remains fragile. This is equally the case in the new countries which have become independent before a national sentiment of unity has developed and which are likely to be more concerned, at least initially, with economic and social advance (or, as in Ghana, with the issue of the security of the leader) than with recognizing the limits written into, or implicit in, their inherited structures of government.

The wide variations in the origins, functions, and strengths of constitutionalism can be illustrated by considering two of its most common and crucial characteristics: the system of fundamental rights and liberties, which embodies some of the most important substantive limitations on power; and constitutional jurisdiction, i.e., action through the courts to secure the observance of the rules of a constitution.

Basic Rights and Liberties Today

Perhaps the outstanding early statement of the fundamental rights and liberties of the citizen is embodied in the American Bill of Rights. But this and similar lists of rights have at times been criticized in this century as being too individualistic, too little concerned with the needs of groups, and too negative—in the sense of emphasizing "freedom from" rather than "freedom to." This last charge reflects the feeling that free speech and protection against arbitrary search and seizure are small comfort to men who are denied the chance to earn a living and to improve their existence. Whether the order of values implicit in such a charge is as self-evident today, when we have again become more sensitive to the supreme value of individual liberty, as it seemed in the interwar period so beset by economic depression, is perhaps open to question. But, in any case, it is true that catalogues of fundamental rights, not only in the sense of protection against governmental action but in other areas—such as the right to work and to decent payment for work, to social security, to education, and other rights characteristic of the welfare state—have been inserted not only in spurious documents like the Stalin Constitution, but also in modern democratic constitutions, i.e., the Weimar Constitution of Germany and the preambles to the Constitutions of the postwar French Fourth Republic and the Republic of India.

To the extent that they express the aspirations of underprivileged groups or classes or of developing nations, the importance of these latter rights is very great. Under such circumstances they can become the clarion calls of political movements, and their political impact may be greater than that of the "old-fashioned" freedoms. The Asian and African masses are often said to be more interested in freedom from want than in more rarefied concepts like freedom of opinion; yet even if this is partially true, most of their leaders, at least, would prefer to combine both.

But the classic individual rights and freedoms retain their value and even gain new luster when people have had the bitter experience of living under totalitarian or authoritarian rule. The loss of freedom makes us appreciate what we too easily take for granted as long as we have it. Life under totalitarian lawlessness teaches people anew the importance of basic personal freedoms, particularly that of legal security in its most elementary sense of freedom from arbitrary arrest and detention. It is significant that the Bonn Constitution has dropped most of the Weimar catalogue of economic and social rights while giving the traditional bill of rights new emphasis. This is true also of the post-Fascist Constitution of Italy.

There are also some new departures in the sphere of the classical freedoms themselves. It is not surprising that in an age of mass society, emphasis should shift somewhat from the traditional political rights to those affecting personal development and cultural expression. Since individuals in a mass society must conform to the standards of mass organization and also must inevitably have less influence over policy decisions, the

meaning of freedom is now also related to the right to noncon-
formity in those areas of life which have not yet been invaded
by the state. Thus, in the United States, there has of late been
interesting debate concerning the protection of the rights of
creative expression in the arts, literature, and the entertain-
ment fields; of the right to be protected against the too pervasive noise of one's environment; of the right of audiences to
refuse to become "captive" victims of advertising; and of the
right of the citizen, in a shrinking and integrated world, to
move freely not only within his own country but in the world
abroad, i.e., freely to leave and re-enter his country.

But the chief field of basic rights remains that of the classical
bills of rights. Through these, from the time of "the mother of
them all," the English Bill of Rights, there have been established not only the basic boundary lines of freedom, but also a
bridge between liberalism and democracy, since without guarantees of some fundamental civil and political rights—the right
to vote, freedom of speech, association, assembly, and the press,
as well as freedom from arbitrary arrest and the right to *habeas
corpus,* that is, for an arrested person to have his case reviewed
publicly before a judge within a limited period of time after
arrest—genuine democracy, in the sense of rule of the people,
would be impossible. What is the present status of these rights
in the major countries?

In the Soviet Union, up to and throughout the era of Stalin,
individual rights were not protected against the state and its
pervasive terror machinery in any meaningful sense of the
words "rights" or "protection." The famous Bill of Rights of the
Stalin Constitution was merely a fig leaf to cover up a dictatorship which, like all modern nondemocratic regimes, seemed unable to dispense with pseudo-democratic trappings. Of what
avail, for instance, were any of the classical freedoms if they
could be exercised only "in conformity with the interests of the

working people"—a conformity that was defined only by the ruling political group?

For the post-Stalinist period, however, the judgment should, perhaps, not be quite so negative. Certainly, we have not yet been given evidence of genuine guarantees of political rights, and it is not easily imaginable that a one-party dictatorship will permit the free formation of competing political associations, or, in a system of state- or party-owned newspapers, provide for meaningful freedom of the press. But we have seen how in the nonpolitical sphere some leeway has more recently been allowed to individual and group expression and activity, and in the field of personal freedom it is difficult to think of widespread arbitrariness, complete with legally unchecked secret police, indefinite detentions in concentration camps, etc., being reintroduced in a nation becoming accustomed to at least a minimal degree of security. The same is true of the social and economic "rights" guaranteed by the Constitution. So widely, and over so long a period, have practices like free education, free health services, etc., been followed on the basis of general laws that—possibly contrary to the intentions and expectations of the original Constitution- and policy-makers—they have for all intents and purposes become irrevocable. It would seem to show that even under authoritarianism, lip-service and paper promises may turn into restraints on rulers who cannot afford to disregard the expectations of a people whom they themselves have educated and "modernized."

On the face of it, the protection of rights and liberties in the United States lies at the opposite pole. Even as compared with other liberal democratic systems, the American system is more fully defined and seems more safely implemented and protected. Rights and liberties are written into both federal and state constitutions, which enjoy the aura of a "higher law." They are protected not only against executive but also against legislative infringement; and independent courts function so as to make observation and enforcement real.

But even in the United States, reality does not always come up to these ideals and potentialities. First of all, there are areas —in the geographical as well as the personal sense—where the enforcement machinery of the state, instead of protecting, turns against the individual to be protected, and the courts are unavailable or ineffective in the face of such abuse. One must, of course, reckon with a certain amount of abuse or neglect under every system, even a liberal-democratic one, but in America the incidence is higher than in other democracies, and this not only in reference to the most obvious case—the Negro in the South. Local and state police authorities and even courts have often been woefully inadequate in the protection of individual and group rights and liberties.

Second, there has been in the United States the impact of special strains and stresses, such as those of the Cold War and its recurrent crises. Certain limitations of political rights are directly traceable to these strains, and some of these limitations may even be necessary, for the ingenious strategies of modern totalitarian movements confront democracies with the dilemma of whether to grant unlimited freedom to enemies who would use it to destroy freedom for others, or whether to restrict freedom and risk a far-reaching curtailment, or at least a dangerous erosion, of liberties. In tending toward the second alternative, the United States has permitted a lessening of political rights by recognizing certain legal limitations on liberties, in particular through a broad construction of the "clear-and-present-danger" test. Without the same justification, and far more dangerous, however, are the extralegal social pressures for conformity. Experience, especially in the period of the McCarthy investigations, shows how dependent are formal guarantees upon public support.

Yet, if at that time fear and pressure for conformism threatened basic rights in the United States, Great Britain offers encouraging evidence on the other side, that is, that continued respect for freedom is itself the best guarantee of basic rights. The preservation of traditional liberties in that country provides a prime illustration of the force of tradition and the prevailing spirit of a nation, as contrasted with the impact of formal rules and institutions. Even though no higher law of a written constitution protects the basic rights of Englishmen, they are safeguarded through the application of the rule of law. While Parliament, by legislation, or the Cabinet, by delegated power, clearly has the power to tamper with personal rights, there is little danger that either would do so more than temporarily, and then only during genuine emergencies. So closely is Britain integrated as a nation of free men mutually tolerant and respectful of their differences that, in Churchill's words, they can "lump" (i.e. swallow, or accept) the most unpleasant of such divergencies. Typical of this attitude was Churchill's comment on the opinions and activities of Hewlett Johnson, the "Red Dean" of Canterbury: "Free speech carries with it the evils of all the foolish, unpleasant, venomous things that are said, but on the whole we would rather lump them than do away with them."

Even Britain, however, politically mature though it be, has its frailties, more noticeable abroad than at home. To the British, basic rights have always been the rights of Englishmen rather than the rights of man. Though the native people of their colonial possessions have received genuine blessings, like the extension of the common law, impartial standards of administration, and sound rules of hygiene and health, they did not often enjoy until late in their development either the political rights or the tolerance of unpopular opinions which are among Britain's most distinguished attributes at home.

In contrast to the British, the French since the age of the Enlightenment and the Great Revolution have raised the battle cry of the "rights of man" rather than the rights of Frenchmen. But the trouble has been that it was the battle cry of only one group of Frenchmen in the perennial French conflict of opposing ideologies. Many a glorious legal and political battle has been fought over these rights and their protection, and some of them have been decisive for the liberal democratic development of the country—as witness the Dreyfus affair, where a long and ultimately successful fight was waged at the turn of the century to clear the name of an unjustly convicted Jewish army officer. But it can hardly be said that these rights are as safely anchored in France as they are in Britain. The French system is at its best in the protection it offers of individual liberties through its system of administrative jurisdiction, but these procedures protect personal rights, such as property rights, against an entrenched and solid bureaucracy, rather than political freedoms. It would be gratifying to infer from the broad freedoms enjoyed in France by political movements of even the most radical sort, including Communism, a British-type agreement on "lumping it" in the interests of freedom and diversity; what seems more likely, however, is that this freedom was the result of dissent and of the weakness of the public power, which asserted itself with difficulty in the face of warring factions.

As for Germany, there (as in France) liberalism has not been unsuccessful in the realm of personal security and property rights; these were clearly protected by that Central European marriage of freedom and authoritarianism known as the *Rechtsstaat*. But political rights and liberties prior to the republican regime of Weimar meant little more than the ventilation of grievances in press or parliament, to which the ruling powers paid scant attention. If the Weimar regime distinguished—and perhaps extinguished—itself through an overly broad grant of political freedoms, the Bonn Constitution also experiments in two novel and interesting ways: first, by declaring that certain very basic rights are unamendable (Article 79), a provision which raises the difficult problem of whether there can and should be limits to the power of constitutional amendment; and second, by setting out limits upon the exercise of political rights when used "in order to attack the liberal-democratic order" (Articles 18, 21). It was under these latter provisions that neo-Nazis and later the Communist Party were suppressed in West Germany. In a country such as Germany, where authoritarianism has been strongly entrenched, there is always a danger of relapse into illiberalism, but in the German case recent experience with the extreme of Nazi oppression seems also to have had the opposite effect, namely, of alerting the public to the dangers inherent in even the beginnings of arbitrariness. Some cautious hope may therefore be drawn from the reaction of the German public (it was public opinion at large rather than that of parliament or executive leadership) to the famous *Spiegel* affair,* i.e., the arrest of publishers and editors of a news magazine who were accused of having revealed military "secrets" that had been widely known and even publicly discussed at that time.

The suppression of the Communist Party in certain countries brings sharply into focus a problem troubling many democratic states: what to do about organized Communist activity in their political life and in their trade unions. In Italy and France, of course, the Communist Party not only is legal but able to attract large numbers of votes; it also retains a strong, even dominant, influence in the trade unions. In Great Britain, no one would suggest action against the small Communist Party, which continues, election after election, to put up candidates, though with conspicuous lack of success. There has been much more concern about the strong and pervasive Com-

---

* See Otto Kirchheimer and Constantine Menges on the *Spiegel* case, in *Politics in Europe,* edited by Gwendolen M. Carter and Alan F. Westin (New York: Harcourt, Brace and World, 1965).

munist influence in some British trade unions, but the problem has been left to the unions themselves, which have ultimately succeeded in limiting the scope of Communist influence. Particularly interesting in this regard is the experience of Australia, whose Liberal administration was returned to office in 1951, largely on a platform of outlawing the Communist Party, an end sought not because the party was strong politically, but because of its dominance within powerful trade unions. The legislation passed to this end was declared unconstitutional by the courts, and the effort was subsequently abandoned. As in Great Britain, however, the Australian unions thereafter made a massive and largely successful effort to rid themselves of Communist control.

More direct attacks on local Communist Parties have been carried out in Canada, the United States, and South Africa. Canada outlawed its Communist Party in the early 1930's, but has not acted against the small Labour Progressive Party that has taken its place. In Quebec, Canada's populous and largely French-speaking province, the notorious Padlock Law of 1937 was used to prevent the holding of meetings suspected of being Communist-oriented, or being otherwise challenging to the restrictive policies of the Duplessis regime, until the law was declared *ultra vires* by the Canadian Supreme Court in 1957.

The United States has extended the clear-and-present-danger test, as we have said, and has used the Smith Act of 1940 to prosecute successfully more than one hundred prominent Communist Party officials on the charge of advocating the overthrow of government by force. Moreover, the Communist Control Act of 1954 prevents the Communist Party from operating, at least in the Federal sphere, as a legal entity, i.e., from putting candidates on a ballot or suing in court. But the American Communist Party has not yet been formally outlawed, so that it may be said to exist in a quasi-legal form. In fact, a small pro-Chinese Communist Party was formed in the United States in 1965 by a dissident faction of the Soviet-oriented Communist Party.

Most far-reaching of such measures is South Africa's Suppression of Communism Act (1950), which made unlawful not only the Communist Party, but any other organization said to promote Communist activities. Under this law, a liquidator is empowered to take over the assets of such organizations and to compile a list of their officeholders or supporters. These persons can then be publicly named and thereafter barred by the government from taking part in any specified organization, to enter or remain in a prescribed area, or to attend any gathering of more than three persons.

It has become clear from the administration of this Act that persons other than Communist Party members can be attacked under its provisions. The Act defines Communism not only as the doctrine of Marxian Socialism expounded by Lenin or Trotsky or any other doctrine which seeks to establish a one-party state based on the dictatorship of the proletariat, but also as any scheme "which aims at bringing about any political, industrial, social or economic change within the Union by the promotion of disturbances or disorder, by unlawful acts or omissions." When this provision was used to convict the leaders of the nonwhite passive disobedience campaign in 1952, the judge termed their offense "statutory Communism." Thus, it is all too apparent how broadly such provisions can be interpreted. Two white members of Parliament, both elected as native representatives by the small African electorate in Cape Province (since 1960, Africans no longer have even this type of representation in the national Parliament), lost their seats, and another former Communist was prevented from running for office; numerous trade-union leaders have been removed from their offices; and almost all the articulate nonwhite leaders have been placed under ban (if not in prison or exile) at one time or another. A Nobel Prize winner, ex-Chief Albert J. Luthuli, has long been restricted to a small area and, with many others, may not be quoted in any South African publication. Few situations point up more clearly the dangers implicit in such broadly worded statutes. Nor is there much evidence here, or elsewhere, that a ban on the Communist Party does much more than drive it underground, a fact pointed up by the South African trial of Communist leaders in 1964–65.

Such a survey as this underlines the fact with which we started—that the response to Communist infiltration and the pressures of the international situation may threaten to erode the protection of traditional and fundamental civil and political rights. In a country like South Africa, where the white minority is outnumbered four to one by the nonwhites, the fear of Communist influence easily becomes intermingled with the potential threat of African nationalism. Even in the United States, and in spite of the formal guarantees of the Bill of Rights, individuals have been convicted and imprisoned on the basis of what they are said to have advocated, rather than because of specific acts committed by them. To safeguard individual rights in the light of such pressures requires not only restraint on the part of government, but also constant alertness by the governed.

CONSTITUTIONAL JURISDICTION

It is common in democratic countries to look on the courts not only as the protectors of individual rights, but also as the agency which ensures that state action will not transgress constitutional limits. "Constitutional jurisdiction," as we have said, means court action to secure the observance of the rules of a constitution. As such, it may attain political importance far beyond that of any other judicial action.

It is hardly surprising that constitutional jurisdiction has been particularly important in countries with a federal structure, such as the United States, Canada, Australia, Switzerland,

West Germany, and Austria. Delimiting the powers of member units in relation to those of the federal (national) unit is vital for the functioning of such a system. It took a civil war in the United States to establish the principle that a judicial organ of the Federal Government rather than an individual state (or states) is the final arbiter. As resistance to the Supreme Court decision in the school segregation cases and the long series of supplementary judgments point up, this principle has to be re-established again and again. Ultimately, history has shown that such delimitations of power depend not only on judicial interpretation, but also on acquiescence by the most powerful forces in a community in the decisions which have been made.

The different ways in which constitutional jurisdiction functions can be illustrated by the experience of three countries where such jurisdiction has assumed major importance: Switzerland, West Germany, and the United States. There are three chief areas in which courts* may undertake to guarantee the functioning of a constitutional system, and each of the countries mentioned illustrates one of them. In the first place, the courts may act to uphold the individual or group rights and liberties which a constitution protects. A second important sphere is the relation between ordinary legislation and the law of the constitution. The third is keeping in balance both the powers of, and the relations between, organs of government, e.g., the spheres of the legislature and executive, the rights of majorities and minorities in a parliament, or the jurisdiction of the federal government and the member states. Accordingly, constitutional jurisdiction may deal with any or all of the following: (a) conflicts between the state and individuals or groups wherein the latter claim there has been a violation of basic rights or liberties; (b) judicial review of the constitutionality of

* Whether constitutional jurisdiction is exercised by the general courts of a country (as in the United States and in Switzerland) or by a special and separate "constitutional tribunal" (as in Germany, Austria, and Italy) is immaterial in this connection.

laws; (c) "organ conflicts," that is, conflicts between the organs of the state or government.

The Swiss system chiefly implements point *a* above. There is in Switzerland no court decision in organ conflicts, and there is no judicial review of federal (in contrast to cantonal) statutes. The chief function of Swiss constitutional jurisdiction, therefore, is the broad protection of individual and group rights in cases of the "constitutional complaint" of citizens. This function reflects a profound concern with the maintenance of a sphere of individual freedom from state interference. In contrast, the distinctive function of the American judicial system (though not, to be sure, its only function, since that system is also concerned with the protection of rights and liberties) is judicial review (point *b* above), i.e., the maintenance of the superiority of the Constitution over all state action, including ordinary lawmaking. This reflects an ingrained American feeling that the Constitution is the higher law, to be preserved against the changing and possibly transitory will of the people.

The new German system, finally, is perhaps most interesting in providing for legal settlement of organ conflicts (point *c*). The idea of offering political groups and governmental authorities a chance to fight out constitutional conflicts legally perhaps reflects a typically German legalistic approach to political problems generally. Moreover, it goes back to the nineteenth-century origin of Continental constitutions in the crown vs. people compromise. Even under the German Empire (when the Bundesrat, the upper chamber, had jurisdiction), and later under Weimar (when a constitutional tribunal was established), provision had been made for the resolution of certain types of organ conflicts. But only now has full "juridification" of the system been attained, with the Bonn Constitution allotting to the Federal Constitutional Court the power to decide even those constitutional conflicts which arise among the highest federal organs and agencies, such as, for instance, between the government and a parliamentary opposition group over the enactment of a law. Here, as well as in the protection of rights and liberties and through judicial review, the new German Constitutional Court has vigorously asserted itself. This, for a country with strong authoritarian traditions, is an important new venture.

What about constitutional jurisdiction in other countries and systems? Totalitarian regimes, of course, cannot permit procedures for the effective limitation of power; they avoid even the make-believe appearance of such jurisdictions, asserting that to give courts powers of judicial review, for instance, would hamstring the sovereign legislature. While in totalitarian systems this attitude simply reflects the determination to keep all power in the hands of the ruling group—the party—it is also true that the French have used the same argument in all sincerity. To the French, who traditionally have believed that sovereignty rests inalienably in the people and its elected assembly, the idea of a higher law of the Constitution is foreign. Nonetheless, the Fifth Republic has established a Constitutional Council which gives advisory, though not binding, rulings on the meaning and relevance of constitutional provisions. The French unitary system leaves no room for federal-state conflicts.

But it would be strange, indeed, to find no institutional protection of individual rights in the very country of the *droits de l'homme et du citoyen,* and we do find such protection in the system of administrative jurisdiction, headed by the Conseil d'État (Council of State), which takes infinite care to protect and indemnify individuals injured by unjust or unfair acts committed by government officials or in the name of the state. Before World War II, it was difficult for private citizens to secure comparable compensation in the United States and Great Britain, but procedures for so doing were established in the United States in 1946 through the Federal Tort Claims Act, and in Great Britain the following year by the Crown Proceedings Act.

The British system of parliamentary supremacy, like the French system, operates without judicial review or judicial settlement of organ conflicts. It is typically British in avoiding the use of special institutions for protection, and in relying instead on such general rules and traditions as the rule of law, the recognition of implied restraints upon state power, and the application of the rule of reason to any and all of the system's manifestations. Thus again, Great Britain illustrates the importance, beyond constitutional procedures and institutional devices, of national tradition for the maintenance of a constitutionalism which is nowhere more safely anchored than in that country.

This may be the place to mention an institution—the office of the *ombudsman*—which does not, strictly speaking, belong in a discussion of constitutional jurisdiction (it is hard to fit it into any one system) but which is illustrative of the inventiveness and ingenuity of democracies in relation to the problem of effectively protecting individual and group rights and liberties against administrative arbitrariness or neglect. First developed in Sweden, this institution spread from there to other Scandinavian countries and, more recently, to New Zealand and West Germany, though in the latter it is limited so far to the protection of enlisted men against abuse in the armed forces. It has been proposed as a safeguard against "administrative lawlessness" in both Great Britain and Canada and, most recently, even in the United States.

The *ombudsman* is elected by parliament, and thus might be considered an instrument of the legislature to supervise and criticize the executive, but in fact he is independent of parties or other political influence. He deals by various means with complaints from the public at large against arbitrary government actions. Publicity may be the most effective of these means, but in Sweden the *ombudsman* may also "institute proceedings before the competent courts against those who, in the execution of their official duties . . . committed an unlawful act or neglected to perform their official duties properly." In the light of the vast and continuous increase of administrative activities and powers, the office of *ombudsman* may be a significant means of protecting the rights of private persons.

INDEPENDENCE OF THE JUDICIARY

Constitutional jurisdiction is not the only device for safeguarding constitutionalism. There is also an essential relationship between constitutionalism and the judicial function in general. The decisive factor here is judicial independence, whose general importance for the maintenance of a democratic system has already been noted. In contrast to police states, where the courts are looked on as instruments of the regime in carrying out its political and general purposes, courts in constitutional systems are separate, independent agencies, bound by their own rules of procedure and determining cases according to publicly known law.

It is through judicial independence (usually guaranteed by the appointment of judges for life or until a certain age, and their irremovability except for moral causes) that Montesquieu's device for the limitation of power has found its last redoubt in countries like Great Britain and France, where little else remains of the separation of powers. Under modern conditions of the welfare state and of government regulation, the separation between the lawmaking and the executive branches may no longer be as feasible or even as desirable as it used to be; but the separation of an independent judiciary from both seems to be the irreducible minimum required for an effective system of limitation of power. The more modern government interferes, administers, and regulates, the more urgent is the need to preserve a check on the way these activities affect individuals and groups. The helplessness of the individual in the absence of such control is all too obvious in systems where the judiciary is either dependent or powerless, whether they be premodern systems with their *lettres de cachet,* or modern totalitarian systems with their knock on the door in the dead of night.

Modern tyranny has given a new perspective to the old charges that bourgeois justice is liable to dispense class justice. British socialists, for instance, used to claim that the British judicial system and the common law itself gave particular advantages to the claims of property. But such charges are today not often heard. For one thing, British courts placed no impediments in the way of Labour's programs after 1945. But far more important has been the terrifying example of those trials in Nazi Germany, the Soviet Union, and the Soviet satellites in which the law was deliberately twisted to entrap the defendant, and in which judges acted as prosecutors and executioners rather than as impartial umpires. In the face of such experience, the independence of the judiciary, known processes of law, and the continuity of principles underlying legal decisions have taken on new importance.

Democracies nevertheless still have their problems. Equal justice under law must, after all, be dispensed by men. The government of laws must forever be government by people applying and interpreting the laws. And human beings, however strong their feeling of independence and security, inevitably have preferred ideals and predilections, and even preconceived ideas and prejudices. An aging judiciary may be behind the times; a judiciary drawn from certain strata or classes may well reflect some caste or class bias. To some extent, and in the long run, even the U.S. Supreme Court "follows the election returns," and while this is reasonable if it means no more than paying attention in a general way to what the people want, it could be dangerous if it were to lead to the abridgment of basic liberties. Moreover, the law itself necessarily reflects class interest where there is class rule, economic interests where such interests prevail in a given society, religious interests where particular denominations or churches predominate. The remedy here, if one is desired, is not a change in the judicial system, but a change in the laws through democratic processes. As for class, personal, or any other bias of the judicial personnel, the remedy is not to render the judiciary more dependent, but constantly to bring about reforms that make such shortcomings less likely, for example, by selecting the German and even the British judiciary from a less narrow class base and by protecting the American judiciary, especially on the state level, from undue party influence such as is apt to result from the election of judges for limited terms.

Entrusting courts with the authority to limit the use of power by other governmental agencies creates particular types of problems. Difficulties arise, for instance, where courts are entrusted with overly political tasks. When, as in the United States, courts are called upon to decide broad issues involving free enterprise versus governmental regulation or racial segregation versus integration through the interpretation of constitutional norms containing general terms like "due process of law" or "equal protection of the law," decisions are bound to go beyond the realm of ordinary interpretation and to involve elements of policy-making. Recognizing this fact, many countries consider certain political questions (such as particular foreign-policy issues in American practice, or *actes de gouvernement,* as in France) as nonjusticiable, that is, as falling outside the jurisdiction of the courts. Of course, decisions in such cases have to be made somewhere. Whether ultimate control is given to a judicial body or to the more political part of the government which is in charge of the particular field seems to be a matter of tradition and convenience. There are problems and advantages, whichever way the matter is handled. Allowing an independent judiciary to settle such issues may create the danger of rendering the judiciary open to charges of being political; but it may offer protection against the concentration or abuse of power elsewhere. Leaving the decision with an executive or a parliament does provide more concentration of authority; but it may be argued that this is the more democratic method, especially where the executive or assembly has a direct mandate from the electorate.

Another problem arises when constitutions undertake to render any and all constitutional conflicts justiciable, that is, to be settled by the courts. The more encompassing the range of what is considered justiciable, the greater the danger that in a conflict involving basic issues of policy or fundamentally opposed forces in state and society, normative judgments will prove unenforceable. It is during those crises of a regime or country which test the very bases of its institutions that constitutionalism is put to its real test. Only a civil war, and not the Supreme Court, was able to resolve the issues of slavery and of state sovereignty in the United States. The Constitutional Court of Weimar Germany was equally unable to enforce its verdict (compromise decision though it was) when antidemocratic forces undertook to destroy the last stronghold of Weimar democracy. In such cases everything depends on whether judicial bodies are backed up by sufficiently strong public determination to uphold the rule of law in this broader sense.

The crucial importance of a sense of restraint on the part of governing groups is well illustrated by the highly complex situation which developed in South Africa over the Nationalist Government's attempts to place the Cape Coloured (mixed blood)—the last nonwhites who were still permitted to vote for the same candidates as were the whites—on a separate voting roll. The Nationalists at first tried to achieve this purpose through ordinary legislation, though the South African Constitution in one of its two entrenched provisions—i.e., protected by special procedures—provides that the voting rights of non-whites in the Cape Province should not be changed except by a two-thirds majority of both chambers meeting in joint session. When the South African Court of Appeals declared the legislation invalid, the Nationalists refused to accept the verdict as a final settlement of the issue and, again by a simple majority, passed an act providing for a High Court of Parliament, consisting of the entire membership of Parliament, which was to take over the power to review legislation from the Court of Appeal. In effect this meant that Parliament assumed the right to validate its own legislation. The appellate court declared this act to be invalid also, since it was clearly designed to serve the purpose of the earlier legislation.

The Nationalists proceeded to make the "sovereignty of Parliament" and the "interference" of the courts issues in the 1953 general election, in which they secured a larger parliamentary majority. Still unable, however, to win the necessary two-thirds majority in the House of Assembly and Senate, the Nationalists moved to more stringent measures. Five new judges were added to the Court of Appeal, and soon afterward a new measure raised the quorum to eleven whenever the Court considers the validity of an act of Parliament. More decisive, in 1955 a new Senate Act increased the size of the second chamber and made provincial representation dependent not on proportionate legislative strength as before, but on majority vote. Under these provisions, the Nationalists controlled seventy-seven votes in the new Senate, as compared with thirty in the old chamber. These additions finally enabled them in mid-1956 to pass their constitutional amendment despite widespread demonstrations against it.

It became obvious in this situation that the South African National Party had no basic sense of constitutionality, such as sparked the vigorous American opposition to the relatively mild "court-packing" proposal of President Roosevelt in 1937, which would have added another judge to the Supreme Court whenever one of those already serving reached the age of seventy-five. Even though he had achieved a remarkable electoral success the year before, Roosevelt felt obliged to bow to the storm of criticism evoked by this scheme and to withdraw it. But in the absence of such a responsive attitude, demonstrations have little effect. Under these circumstances, the South African opposition to Nationalist expedients could have been effective only if it had been ready to resort to forcible measures, which might conceivably have led to a clash of arms. Natural reluctance to go that far, plus the fact that the opposition lacked a sense of personal commitment to the group that was being deprived of its rights, and even perhaps to the Constitution, which was a compromise between racial groups rather than a symbol of unity, led to an ultimate acquiescence in the situation by white South Africans (who hold the monopoly of political power). By so doing, however, the opposition left the way open for subsequent measures which imperil the rule of law. To lose the safeguard of established rules of procedure as limitations on the power of the parliamentary majority is to make possible the uncertainties of arbitrary rule.

DECONCENTRATION OF POWER

So far we have been considering the limits which are placed on government through the protection of individual rights, the restraints of the constitution, and the functional division of powers between the executive, legislature, and judiciary. It is now time to look in some detail at the territorial division of power, or at least of responsibility, which is provided by local government and by federalism. Historically, the limitations upon the authority of a central government which are imposed by deconcentration developed long before constitutional and legal limitations. The "absolute" monarchies of prerevolutionary Europe, for instance, were much less absolute in practice than they claimed to be in theory. This was simply because the central government was not then technically equipped to deal with local matters in remote parts of the country. Today, national government, and especially national administration, is so organized that it can and usually does operate side by side with the organs of local and of intermediate units of government even in the most remote places. In fact, the distinctive feature of a federation, in contrast to a confederation, is that national law is operative throughout the country. The expansion of national functions and responsibilities, however, endangers the functioning of those local and possibly regional levels of government which used to enjoy virtual autonomy, and thus removed whole areas from the influence of the central government.

Local Self-Government

Traditionally, one of the counterweights against too much centralized government was found in local self-government. It is often said, and with some justice, that the "grass roots" of democracy, its essential training ground, are to be found at the local level, where people deal with problems of immediate and direct importance to themselves—problems, moreover, which are intelligible to them in terms of their personal experience. Significantly, local government in Germany developed and was able to gain genuine importance at a time when German state institutions were still authoritarian; again, after the German collapse at the end of World War II, self-government first reasserted itself at the local level. Not only have local self-governing institutions shown stubborn vitality in times of stress; they can also provide a healthy counterbalance to overcentralization, restraining the "apoplexy at the center and the anemia at the extremities" which are always threats in the highly organized, bureaucratic state of today.

It must be admitted, however, that even in countries with long traditions of local self-government, there is a marked trend toward looking on local government as a device for mere decentralization rather than as a counterbalance to the central administration. In Britain, for instance, many activities, such as education and public health, which used to be locally inspired are now organized on a national scale; genuine self-government on the local level thus threatens to become a casualty of the welfare state.

Yet there still is a marked difference between the British and American systems of local government and that of the French. In France, the authority of the prefect remains supreme within the department, the largest of the local divisions; but the prefect is the political agent of the central administration. In Britain and the United States, however, local officials are employed and paid by the local units, even though in many cases they must meet national or state-imposed standards.

The most serious evidence of decline in the vitality of local government in many countries is the lack of interest in local issues. In France, Britain, and Germany, for instance, local elections are increasingly looked on as trials of strength for the national parties, which interject national issues into local contests. Although this somewhat increases public interest, it also entails the danger that political contests, like administrative programs, are merely being decentralized and have no firm roots in local needs. In this perspective, the localism of American politics may appear to have more merit than is commonly recognized.

There is one problem the world over which may yet prove to pose the gravest threat to meaningful local government in the traditional sense: the trend not only toward urbanization but toward the formation of huge metropolitan areas, the "megalopolises" of the future, sheltering tens of millions of people and covering vast continuous territory cutting through old local government areas or even boundaries of "states" (in the United States or Germany) or similar political units. This development poses a twofold problem: how to bring even issues of "local" character close to individuals who are mere atoms in such huge communities, and how to coordinate the affairs of a megalopolis which, in terms of government and administration, is cut up among a large number of units. Much in the solution of the most urgent problems facing the urbanized mankind of the future—such as traffic and transportation, decent housing and education, public health and the pollution of our environment—will depend on a new approach to such new-style problems of local government.

Federalism

Federalism is a much more effective means of providing deconcentration of authority than local government, since it establishes constitutional arrangements allocating power to the regional as well as to the national governments. One of the important functions of the constitutional jurisdiction of the courts in countries like the United States, Canada, Australia, Germany, Switzerland, or Nigeria, where a federal division of power exists, is to watch over the delimitation of the powers of both the central authority and the component units, as we have noted, and to afford protection to their continued existence and spheres of action whenever a relevant case raises the issue. Yet although this safeguard exists, the problems encountered in local government also appear to some extent where federalism provides an intermediary level of government between local and central affairs.

Even in the classical federal systems, whether in the largest or in one of the smallest democracies in the world—the United States and Switzerland—there is now a serious question whether units below the national government which are not mere administrative subdivisions of that government can effectively carry out more than strictly local functions in a period when so many activities are necessarily nationwide, if not still broader. Both national planning and national security are necessarily functions of the national government, and these activities tend to become ever more encompassing. Switzerland even amended its Constitution in 1947 in order to enlarge the jurisdiction of the federation in economic matters. The fact that only the federal government can command the resources to finance large-scale development programs and social welfare has greatly strengthened the position of the national administrations of Australia and to a lesser, though still considerable degree, of Canada. Thus, there is a marked trend toward centralism in the older, established federal systems of the world.

In the face of this development, students of federalism have given much thought to its inherent constitutional and political problems. There is a long series of classical problems of federalism. Should the federal or state sphere possess those unspecified residual powers that exist? Should the administration of national laws be entrusted to national executive agencies, as in the United States, or should it be carried on in the main through state bureaucracies but under federal supervision, as in Germany and Switzerland? The same question arises, be it noted, in respect to the organization of the judiciary: Should there be, on the American pattern, two parallel columns of courts reaching from bottom to top in both the federal and the state spheres; or, as in Europe, Australia, and Canada, state judiciaries coordinated by one federal supreme court? Finally, there is the question of how best to organize that body which in federal structures customarily represents the member units on the federal level of government. Is it better to follow the American or Australian senatorial systems, where delegates to the second chamber are representatives of the people, and elected by their votes; or, as might seem theoretically closer to the idea of federalism, to have the delegates represent the state units, i.e., their governments, on the German pattern?

All of these questions in turn are influenced by broader underlying forces and trends. While, for instance, the unit which enjoys unlisted (i.e., undefined) residual powers might seem to have the advantage, the real balance depends on how broadly the listed ("enumerated") powers are in practice defined and applied. In Canada, where residual powers were vested in the central government, judicial decisions by the Privy Council long acted to build up the separate jurisdictions of the provinces. In contrast, American constitutional history serves to show how terms like "interstate commerce" may be used to enhance central power at the expense of the member units, despite the vesting of residual powers in the latter. What really counts is the viability of the member units, which today is determined by two major factors: financial and political.

The political factor resolves itself into the question of whether genuine and sufficiently strong social, economic, and cultural interests, possibly backed up by regionally concentrated national, linguistic, or religious groups, seek protection from centralization through reinforcing states' rights. Financial viability depends on the distribution of the chief financial resources, especially taxes. Even constitutional systems like the Australian and the German, which began by reserving most of the sources of income for the states, have ended by giving the federal government the major share of financial powers and resources. In countries like the United States, where, constitutionally, there is free competition between levels of government in tapping resources, the balance of income and expenditures has likewise shifted overwhelmingly to the national level.

Even more relevant than the financial factor to the survival and viability of federalism is whether or not strong sentiments of regionalism exist. There is in this respect a striking contrast between old-established systems, such as the United States and the European federal states, and the new countries of the world. In the old federal countries, with the possible exception of Canada and Switzerland, one gains the impression that strongly felt regionalism is largely obsolescent. As distances shrink in the air age, as metropolitan areas cut through state lines, and as people move like latter-day nomads from place to place, the traditionalist, partly nonrational, regional sentiment which underlies genuine federalism tends to diminish and, indeed, to atrophy. It has even been claimed that federalism has become largely irrelevant or inapplicable because of the jet plane, the superhighways, and the instant communications systems of our technological age, and that these and similar factors serve to render even nation-states, at any rate the smaller ones among them, out of date.

It is nevertheless true in the older federal countries that certain interests which by themselves have little to do with regionalism have tried to underpin federal divisions. Thus, in Germany, national political parties find their control of state governments a vantage point from which to influence national policies. In Austria, the Social Democratic Party, whose doctrine is centralist rather than federalist, is strongly entrenched in the member unit of Vienna and for this reason defends the Austrian federal system; so does its chief opponent, the People's Party, which controls the rural and Alpine states. In the United States, mining, gas, oil, and similar interests may become more influential by virtue of their dominant position in particular states and their consequent influence on those states' senators in Washington, and thus be more ardent supporters of federalism. The American party system as such, of course, is still built on local and regional organizations. But none of this evidences strong regional feelings among the people as a whole —feelings which do not in fact exist, except for white sectionalism in the South.

Canada is somewhat different because of French-speaking Quebec, with its recently resurgent spirit of nationalism and separatism, sparked by local pride and economic aspirations. Moreover, the Canadian provincial units are far larger and more distinctive than are American states. More particularly, Canadian federalism has been reinforced not only by judicial interpretations, as we have seen, but also by the not-infrequent practice of the electorate of choosing different parties to control provincial administrations from those they support nationally—probably for the very purpose of maintaining some territorial checks and balances to powerful national parties.

Nevertheless, regardless of local situations, the issues represented by political parties in the older, established states are national, as, inevitably, are the interests and organizations of the chief social and economic groups (labor, trade, and industry) in industrial countries. This is probably the chief reason why the new federalism written into Italy's postwar constitution remained a dead letter, with the possible exception of two regions: Sicily and the (formerly Austrian) Alto Adige.

In regions such as these, federalism still seems to have some genuine regional backing in the sense of a feeling that nationality, language, or general historical background sets them apart from other groups or from the majority population. The basis for the different status of Scotland and Wales in Britain (which, of course, is not federalism) is not entirely dissimilar. Quebec in Canada, Bavaria in Germany, Catalonia and the Basque regions in Spain before the Franco dictatorship did away with their autonomy, reflect the same distinctiveness. With industrialization, some of these differences are gradually being overlaid, but, as Quebec demonstrates, this process does not necessarily eliminate either an insistence on local autonomy or strains within a federation.

On the whole, however, the outlook for federalism in the older systems is none too good. But this does not necessarily pose a threat to liberalism. It is far from certain that smaller units of government are more sensitive to the rights and liberties of individuals and groups than are larger ones. In the United States it is quite the other way around as far as the protection of the rights of racial minorities and people of color are concerned. Moreover, central government at times provides more effective protection against the pressure of nongovernmental power, such as that of "big business" or other special-interest groups. In any event, some kind of administrative decentralization will undoubtedly be retained in many spheres of activity in order to lessen the burden on national administrations.

If, in the democracies, federal divisions are becoming less important, in the dictatorships they are simply irrelevant. Although the Soviet Union is technically a federation, the division of power is far more apparent than real. In Khrushchev's Russia, responsibilities between the national and regional spheres were shared much more than they were under Stalin. But the essential characteristics of both the Soviet and the Nazi systems demand the concentration of power in one man or in a small group backed by a monolithic party which permeates all operations throughout the country. The very fact that Soviet policy has repeatedly gone from centralism to greater decentralization and back again testifies to the inherent weakness of federalism under such conditions.

In Latin America, too, federalism (largely copied from the United States), is often simply make-believe, even where there is no dictatorship. Its general weakness in reflected in the ready resort to "federal intervention," which substitutes federal for regional control in the member units.

On the other hand, federalism seems to have particular importance today in nations which have only recently, or are about to, come into existence. When large units gain their independence from colonial rule, federalism may be the only way to prevent their disintegration into nonviable linguistic or similar fragments. India, whose federalism now reflects its wide range of linguistic groups, retained its unity only by yielding to their demands for separate divisions. The trend toward further subdivisions may, however, call forth a counteracting trend, with centralism enforced in the interests of maintaining unity. This happened in Indonesia, which was transformed from a federation into a centralized republic soon after gaining independence.

Federalism provides an obvious means whereby diverse or small units can group themselves into viable or even powerful entities. The United States provides the earliest illustration of this process. The Canadian and the Australian colonies also took this route to national unity and statehood between 1867 and 1901. In Nigeria, with its 55 million people, federal association has proved capable of holding together three widely different though economically complementary regions, each with a dominant tribal group—Yoruba in the west, Ibo in the east, and Hausa-Fulani in the numerically strongest north—as the country moved toward and then achieved independence in 1960. That the Nigerian Federation has suffered severe strains since that time is less significant than the fact that it has weathered them. The Malaysian Federation, another recent addition to the independent members of the Commonwealth of Nations, is a further example of how the federal form has combined self-conscious, and in this instance separated, smaller entities. Despite its dispersed and varied units, Malaysia has exhibited considerable cohesion in the face of overt interference by Indonesia. A no less striking example of the usefulness of the federal form is provided by the Cameroun Federal Republic, which comprises a territory formerly held under trusteeship by France and one formerly under British supervision. Thus, federalism can provide a framework for experimentation and a flexibility in determining the allocation of power that help to make its form suitable to widely varying conditions.

If federalism can play this role in the making of new nations and thus provide the middle way between splinter units and excessive centralization, it may yet come to play an even larger role in international relations. The increasing interdependence of countries in the field of security and the progressive economic integration of the world may, in the long run, suggest the value of a federal relation to countries with small resources and extensive needs of development. This would be particularly appropriate in West Africa, Equatorial Africa, and East Africa, where the race for independence has brought a number of relatively small countries a political status which their immature economies can barely support.

It must be said, however, that in many areas national and territorial sensitivities and aspirations—either of the territorial unit, or of a particular group within it—have complicated or prevented the progress toward or consummation of a formal federation. The Federation of Rhodesia and Nyasaland, founded in 1953, failed to secure the allegiance and support of its majority Africans and broke into the original component parts: Southern Rhodesia (now called Rhodesia, which has aspirations to independent status under the control of its white minority on the South African pattern), Northern Rhodesia (which in 1964 became independent Zambia) and Nyasaland (which in 1963 became independent Malawi). The West Indies Federation also broke up, though through local jealousies and even miscalculation rather than any problem of racial discrimination. Several attempts at federation in African-controlled Africa have also ended in failure: notably the Mali Federation of Senegal and Soudan, the latter now named Mali; and the projected East African Federation of Uganda, Kenya, and Tanganyika (in 1964 joined with Zanzibar to form Tanzania). Thus federalism can only be an answer to diversity when the units make a concerted and sustained effort to make it so.

Nonetheless, not only the new countries of Africa, but possibly far older ones, too, may ultimately recognize the value of a federal relationship. Even industrial nations, such as Germany, France, and Italy are tending toward such association under the impact of their ever-closer economic and even cultural ties. Indeed, the more audacious might look forward to seeing in the far distant future federalism used as a device to integrate the major powers whose basis of genuine independence has disappeared along with their former "impenetrable" frontiers, and perhaps even to seeing, beyond this, a world federal structure.

V

CHANNELS OF POLITICAL ACTION: ELECTIONS, POLITICAL PARTIES, AND LEGISLATURES

Although constitutions form the framework within which governments should operate, they cannot of themselves answer the most vital question for a democratic state: How is government to be kept responsive to the popular will? It is still possible in a New England town meeting to bring together the citizens to make their own decisions on policy, as Athenians used to do in classical times. But national populations are far too large and too dispersed in modern times for such direct action (even though the device of a national plebiscite is occasionally used, as in Switzerland in both the legislative process and that of constitutional amendment, or as in Australia in the latter). Modern government thus is representative government. But this very fact raises a vast number of other questions: How are representatives to be chosen so that they will be responsible to their constituents? How can they make their influence effective on the executive? In other words, how can the vast variety of often opposing groups in a modern community be linked effectively with the process of government in such a way that policy-making can be carried on speedily and decisively, and yet with due regard to the consent of the governed?

THE PROCESS AND PURPOSE OF ELECTIONS

The most obvious point at which citizens directly influence the conduct of government is at the moment of elections; the

99

63824

most obvious center of representation is the legislature. Through elections, democracies can achieve that peaceful change of administration which is the most difficult of problems for dictatorship. Through legislatures, the public is kept informed of proposals for policy and lawmaking and hears them thrashed out in the battle of conflicting points of view. Moreover, through investigations—either by legislative committees as in the United States, or by the more flexible method of the parliamentary question—the executive may be kept under supervision even on points of administrative detail.

To say this, however, is not to answer a long series of questions, some of them substantive and some technical, but all revolving around these issues: How can representatives be kept responsible both to their own constituents and to the interests of the whole electorate? Whom should representatives represent, and how should they perform this function? And how should elections be conducted and on what electoral basis?

To be more specific: Should elections be held in single-member districts where the decision is always clear, or in multi-member constituencies where the results, through proportional distribution of seats, more nearly reflect the popular vote? Part of the advantage of voting in single-member districts is that the contest is understandable and often dramatic, as in any race where only one person can win. Moreover, in this kind of voting there is no question but that the elected representative is directly responsible to a particular constituency as well as to the whole country in general. In addition, and very important, there is the fact that under this system powerful parties tend, at least in Anglo-Saxon countries, to win so high a proportion of the seats in the legislature that they easily fill the competitive roles of government and opposition. This makes for effective government, since the party in power has the votes to carry out its program; at the same time, the opposition becomes responsible for the clear presentation of alternative policies and for unremitting efforts to keep the government sensitive to its responsibilities.

The problem of single-member constituencies is that the minority stands in danger of being disenfranchised. Beyond the apparent injustice that up to 49 per cent of those who exercise their franchise may not have their voices count in the final selection of the representatives, the presence of third-party candidates, not so rare these days in either Great Britain or Canada, may split the vote, so that the representative is chosen by as few as 34 per cent of the electors. Should there, therefore, be multimember districts and a system of proportional representation, so that minorities will be represented in proportion to their strength throughout the country? Proportional representation may mean voting for a list of party nominees from which the top names are selected in accordance with the number of votes the party secures; or using the single transferable vote, in which the elector ranges his candidates in order of preference and has his second choice counted if his first choice has either been elected already by other people's votes or stands no chance of being elected; or be combined with a final contest between two candidates selected through a "run-off" preliminary contest (as was done during the Third French Republic), in which case the second contest may be open to new entrants or restricted to the two highest winners of the first (in the latter instance often giving rise to political machinations and "deals" among the various parties); or some other procedure. Regardless of details, the results of this system may seem to be fairer than those of contests in single-member constituencies. If Great Britain, for example, used proportional representation, the Liberal Party would have many more members in Parliament, for its proportion of the total vote is nearly always much higher than its proportion of MP's.

But this system also may give rise to several problems. The elections under proportional representation are not so easy to follow as the other type. Nominations, especially under the "list" system of PR (as proportional representation is commonly called), may become the preserve of entrenched party elites or bosses, over which even the party "people" have very little influence. Moreover, under PR it is much more difficult to determine that highly important question in a democratic system: To whom is the representative responsible? Since proportional representation also tends to maximize the voting power of small, closely knit minorities, it tends to split the legislature into so many parties that effective government becomes difficult, if not impossible.

A considerable number of countries, especially smaller ones, have long used, or are now using, one or another form of proportional representation, e.g., Israel, Ireland as well as other small European countries, and Australia, which uses PR for electing the ten senators from each of its six states. West Germany's somewhat complicated election system comes close to being proportional. Most of the larger modern democracies, however, seem to feel that the liabilities of PR outweigh its advantages for choosing the members of the body which is usually the seat of political power—the lower house.

Some countries which do adhere to the system of proportionality have tried to eliminate some of its shortcomings through special devices. In West Germany, for instance, a "5-per-cent clause" denies any representation in the legislature to parties failing to poll a minimum of 5 per cent of the votes. This has successfully prevented the formation of splinter groups; perhaps even too successfully, because as a result, all but two or three parties have tended to disappear from the political arena. Thus, as under the single-member district system, voters rally to only the largest groups, perhaps in part to "climb on the bandwagon." From the point of view of proportionality, this may be regrettable. It provides compensation, however, through the greater stability inherent in a system of a few large parties.

Under the majoritarian principle, which underlies the idea and practice of democracy, every vote should have equal weight (with the one major exception that in federal systems the second chamber representing member states, if composed of popularly elected representatives, may reflect the equality of such member states through an equal number of delegates for each, regardless of population). Few electoral systems, however, make any attempt to satisfy this concept of equality in an exact mathematical manner. But where discrepancy becomes too great, serious problems arise. Even so democratic a system as the British permitted double voting on the basis of special claims to representation—i.e., the university vote and the business-premises vote—until the end of World War II, when the Labour government abolished it.

The most frequent cause of inequality in the actual weight of votes, however, has been malapportionment of districts and failure to reapportion them over long periods of time and after great shifts in population (in recent times generally from the countryside to metropolitan areas). Thus in most countries with single-member districts there are fewer voters in rural than in urban constituencies. This fact grossly exaggerated the political influence of American rural areas until forced "redistricting" under a Supreme Court mandate began to make representation of rural and urban areas more equitable. In South Africa, these inequities still provide a major advantage to the rural constituencies whose voting population is mainly Afrikaner.

Apart from nondemocratic arguments (such as that people "closer to the soil" were more valuable than the "urban rabble," or that educated persons should have stronger influence over political affairs), inequality, especially of rural and city areas, used to be justified by the argument that scattered communities covering large areas should have a measure of compensation. This argument is hardly valid any more in days of rapid communication, but it is still used by strongly entrenched political and economic interests which profit from the system. Thus in the United States, many districts became drastically unequal in size, and in regard to state legislatures electoral provisions would even guarantee by statute that the rural population receive greater representation than urban voters. Since redistricting in the United States was under the control of the self-same bodies whose members were interested in the continuation of this situation, namely, the legislatures, it was not possible to remedy it until the courts intervened. After having refused over a long period of time to go into this "politically sensitive" matter, the Supreme Court reversed itself, and in 1962, in *Baker* v. *Carr,* declared that denial of equal voting rights through malapportionment was irreconcilable with equality before the law as guaranteed by the United States Constitution. This case referred to one chamber of state legislatures, but subsequent decisions have extended the principle to state second chambers as well as to the House of Representatives on the Federal level.

Important shifts in the power structure of the United States can be expected in consequence of this judgment by the court, illustrating once more the frequently decisive role played by constitutional jurisdiction. The reapportionment issue in America also raises the basic question of whether even a majority should have the right to deprive all the citizens of equal representation. Such an attempt has been made by certain states, which tried to salvage the system of unequal districts through a plebiscitary vote on the question. The Supreme Court, however, taking its liberalism in this sphere seriously, has decided that the minority disfavored by such a majority vote must be protected in its right to an equal vote and thus declared the results of such plebiscites to be inadmissible.

In Great Britain and many other countries, the responsibility for redistricting is "depoliticized" by vesting it in impartial bodies such as commissions of judges. While this has had salutary effects in Britain, the effort of South Africa to keep redistricting constantly abreast of changing population levels has created its own problems, since the boundaries of constituencies have been redrawn after every five-year census, and thus between each major election. Such frequent changes (as has also been true of British redistricting since World War II) tend to break down that sense of community within a constituency which contributes so much to the reality of representation. On the other hand, where redistricting lags behind changes in population, there is the opposite, and perhaps even greater, evil of districts becoming drastically unequal as the result of population shifts.

Even with their extraordinarily frequent redistricting, the South African election returns do not follow the popular vote with any degree of exactitude. The Nationalist Party did not poll over 50 per cent of the votes until the republic referendum of 1960 and the general election of 1961, though in 1958 it won 103 out of 156 seats in the House of Assembly. This discrepancy is partly the result of overweighting the rural vote, but it results more directly from a phenomenon also observable in British elections: the fact that a major party (in South Africa the United Party, and in Great Britain the Labour Party) can pile up such huge majorities in urban centers that it "wastes" many of its votes. In fact, redistricting in South Africa has seemed deliberately aimed at massing the opposition vote within constituency boundaries under the principle of similarity of interests, thereby reducing the number of close election contests and causing Parliament to look like a reflection of regional differences and of rural or semi-urban and urban divisions.

What seems evident from this brief survey is that there exists no electoral system which exactly reflects popular views and divisions. This in itself is not necessarily a cause for concern. What is important is to secure a rough approximation of popular sentiment through means which the public accepts as legitimate. Thus, democratic states do not need to worry about attempting to provide any exact mathematical reflection of the electorate—an attempt doomed to failure before it is begun—nearly so much as about obvious subterfuges to secure the advantage of particular groups (such as gerrymandering the boundaries of constituencies), since this undercuts the sense of legitimacy which makes the public trust electoral results.

Even when, as in France under the Fourth Republic, it was the center parties upholding constitutional government which devised electoral rules to their own advantage, they were threatening the system they hoped to save. This danger has also not been absent from postwar Germany and Italy, since the method of election, not being specified in their constitutions, could be devised anew by parliament for each election. Election systems have therefore tended to depend on the calculations of parties or majorities as to which rules would serve them best, and thus have tended to become the football of party politics. Since powerful groups are tempted to abuse their power to disenfranchise small ones, such tactics inevitably help alienate parts of the electorate. For the moment the result might be to the advantage of stable government. But since the process of election is designed to provide representation with the aura of legitimacy, any drastic attempt to distort electoral provisions to the advantage of any group cannot but imperil the faith of the electorate in the democratic system as such.

In the new states of Africa, universal franchise is looked on, not surprisingly, as the key to political power. Where white minorities have long held control, as in South Africa and in Southern Rhodesia, the vote is the means of maintaining or securing power (as, indeed, it still is in parts of the South in the United States). The old conflict between education and economic standing, on the one side, and numbers, on the other, which was waged in earlier days in Western industrializing countries, now permeates the multiracial states, and in a more virulent form. No one can doubt that ultimately numbers will secure the influence in Africa they have elsewhere—the political egalitarianism of the democratic creed is too widely accepted elsewhere to be denied indefinitely there—but this is only the first step. The franchise can put people into power. It is far more difficult to ensure their continuing awareness of and responsiveness to the public will. This is particularly true in Asian and African countries which as yet have had little democratic experience, though at least some of them e.g., India and Nigeria, have demonstrated that illiteracy is no bar to selecting their representatives, and particularly their leaders, shrewdly. Yet not only in the new countries, but also in the older democratic states the issue remains: how to maintain a genuine link between representatives and those who put them into office.

There is, in fact, no real sense in which one man elected by universal suffrage can be said to represent the interests and wishes of all the voters in his constituency, or even the majority of them. The best that he can do, whether he is in the British House of Commons, the American Congress, or the Nigerian or Indian legislature, is to be aware of the most deeply felt preferences of his constituents, to be responsive to the views of important individuals, and to keep in mind the interests of the most important pressure groups operating in his constituency, if indeed they can be reconciled. But still more important are the demands of his party, the activities of its leaders, and his own sense of responsibility for viewing issues in the light of public interest rather than the more narrowly conceived advantages of particular groups or places.

In this framework, what distinguishes democratic government is not that it is representative but that it is responsible. The highest voting records have been those in the Soviet Union, Fascist Italy, and Hitler Germany; but since there is only one slate of candidates, the effect is merely, and inevitably, to endorse the existing regime and in no sense to check its use of power. Democratic states naturally encourage wide use of the franchise and some, like Australia and Belgium make voting compulsory under penalty of a fine. The significance of an election, however, does not lie in the number of people voting, but in the acceptance of this process as the legitimate means of putting a government into or out of office without violence and thereby keeping it responsible to the electorate.

POLITICAL PARTIES

Political parties are the indispensable links between the people and the representative machinery of government. Their role is most obvious when an election is in prospect, but, in fact, they need to be continually operative if a democratic system is to work effectively. It is political parties that organize the vastly diversified public by nominating candidates for office and by popularizing the ideas around which governmental programs are built. They are the vehicles through which individuals and groups work to secure political power and, if successful, to exercise that power. What differentiates political parties from interest or pressure groups is the breadth and variety of their followings and the orientation of their programs toward issues of concern to the whole country. Because awakening interest in these broader questions is a more difficult task than stimulating interest in matters that obviously affect the business or family of an individual, parties must make people politically conscious, i.e., aware of their role as citizens. This role cannot be fulfilled simply by voting, but must be a continuous one if government is to be kept responsive to public interests. Thus, political parties are responsible for maintaining a continuous connection between the public and those who represent it either in the government or in the opposition.

Contrast Between Democratic and Dictatorial Parties

Dictatorships also find the political party an indispensable instrument, but they use it in a very different way than do democracies. Where democratic political parties consciously emphasize diversity and mutual criticism, the political party in the Communist or Fascist dictatorship is the body of the faithful dedicated to maintaining the one truth which their leaders avow. Whereas, apart from their elected members, democratic political parties are informal, nongovernmental organizations (though their activities frequently are carried on within a network of governmental regulations), the dictatorial political party permeates every governmental as well as nongovernmental activity and is virtually a part of the administration it dominates. Where democratic systems maximize opportunities for criticism and protect individual rights to free speech, dictatorial systems operate on the principle of "democratic centralism," i.e., that comments may be offered only in the early stages of a proposal, but once the leaders have made their decision everyone must accept it. Where democracies anticipate an alternation of leaders and provide the public with a choice of candidates for office, dictatorial leaders are self-selected through a power struggle within the party machinery itself. Where democracies use the fervor and slogans of an electoral campaign to publicize the differences between party programs, the party in a dictatorial state carries on continual propaganda campaigns in support of the government's objectives and is the chief means by which conformity is maintained throughout the society.

It is thus confusing and, in a sense, inappropriate, to use the term "political party" both for the competing political associations in democratic states and also for that group which has the full monopoly of political as well as all other powers in a dictatorial totalitarian state. Such a group owes the designation "party" merely to the fact that, in predictatorial times, it actually had been one of several competing political groups on the political scene, from which, subsequently, all but this one disappeared, leaving the now official or "state" party in control of political life. A prime characteristic of political parties as they have evolved in democratic countries is that they are voluntary groupings acquiring their cohesion from perceived and accepted purposes. Democratic political parties also socially integrate the people within their ranks by giving them a common objective and a common organization. But the political party in such states is a vehicle to be used by its members, not a master to give them orders. In totalitarian states, in contrast, the political party is the chief means of control throughout the state, and thus its membership is carefully sifted to ensure conformity to the overriding purpose of the small ruling group. Usually, therefore, its membership is intentionally kept small (in the Soviet Union, for instance, to something like 5 per cent of the population), while it is, of course, the purpose of a party in a democracy to attract as many members as possible. To a certain degree, the totalitarian political party serves the purpose of expressing the sentiments of its members, but only to the degree that is useful for the purposes of the regime. In no case does it act to restrain the exercise of power. As the Nazis used to put it: in democracies authority comes from below and responsibility from above; in dictatorships authority comes from above and responsibility from below.

The Totalitarian Party in a Democratic State

The fundamental differences between democratic- and totalitarian-minded parties raise particular problems when one of the latter is operating within a democratic state. At the beginning of the century, Lenin taught his Bolsheviks the secret of successful subversion: to be a highly organized, highly disciplined group giving unquestioned obedience to its leaders in tactics, in their interpretation of Marxist dogma, and in their objective of radically reorganizing society. Hitler used much the same techniques in building his Nazi party into an instrument capable of taking over power from the Weimar Republic. Thus, fascist and Communist parties are understandably suspected of seeking to overthrow the legitimate government of the country within which they work, and replacing it, if necessary by force, with their own control—either in their own interests or, in the case of a Communist Party, their own as well as the interest of a leading Communist-controlled country: the Soviet Union or China.

Totalitarian-minded parties are most effective in seizing control within states whose machinery of government is weak and indecisive and whose population has little sense of common unity. But even without the hope of replacing the legitimate government with their own, totalitarian-minded parties can do much to disturb the smooth functioning of the state. In France, the Communists regularly polled 25 to 30 per cent of the vote, and until the establishment of the Fifth French Republic sent a large number of their representatives to Parliament. In Italy, much the same has happened. This process has two debilitating effects on democratic operations: It keeps a large number of voters from supporting democratically inclined parties and forces them to compete within the restricted milieu of perhaps 70 per cent of the politically conscious public; and it places a strong group of deputies in a position where they can constantly harass the administration and thus divert it from its primary job of providing effective, responsible government.

The Communist vote in France and Italy does not reflect a comparable degree of mass support. In each case, there is a relatively small, highly organized group of militants who are dedicated to Marxism-Leninism, and a much larger number of people whose grievances these militants exploit by playing on the strains caused by every imaginable shortcoming of the respective society, economy, or political system—such as rising costs of living, unattractive labor conditions in industry, corruption or high-handedness of the civil service, or, particularly in the case of Italy, the misery, backwardness, and exploitation of the farmers. But usually, as long as there is no chance of their securing political power, Communist parties do not seem capable of securing majority support. This is part of the reason why Communists joined in French Popular Front governments, as under Léon Blum in the mid-thirties, and after World War II, but in each case the ultimate awareness of their democratically minded partners that the Communists were seeking their own advantage rather than that of the whole country led to their ejection.

Still more complicated have been the situations in regard to the Communist Party in India. As the only organized group endorsing the Indian war effort (which it did because the Soviet Union was involved), the Communist Party had special opportunities to develop during World War II. Shortly thereafter, and for the first two years of India's independence, the Communists were revolutionary in aims and action. Dealt with firmly by Pandit Nehru's government, the Communist Party then announced that it accepted the democratic framework and would secure its purposes through the peaceful winning of elections. Although the Congress Party has maintained its predominant position in India, as we have noted, the Communists formed the second largest party in Parliament until 11 of their 32 members broke away in September, 1964, after a general split in the party, impending since 1959, and made formal with the creation of a new left-wing, pro-Chinese party known as the Communist Party (Marxist-Leninist).

Defections also occurred in state assemblies, particularly in Andhra, West Bengal, and Kerala. In Kerala, the Communists had earlier scored an electoral victory and been dislodged only when anti-Communist groups through passive-resistance techniques created enough disorder so that the national government exercised its constitutional right to take over the state administration. In 1960, the Congress Party had re-established its electoral majority, but in March, 1965, a split in the local group—which some observers fear presages the disintegration of the national Congress Party—led to a drop from 64 to 36 seats in the 133-member state legislature, while the pro-Peking Communists won 40. Since three-quarters of the left-wing Communists were in jail and the total percentage of votes polled by both Communist Parties was 27, while the Congress parties won 33, the former seem unlikely to take over in Kerala, any more than in the country as a whole, but the splits on both sides make the maintenance of stable democratic government in India still more difficult.

Because of the fear of Communist infiltration, some states, in particular South Africa and West Germany, as we have seen, have outlawed their Communist Parties. But this tactic runs the danger either of forcing the organization underground, where it may be still more dangerous or, as in South Africa, of using broadly phrased anti-Communist legislation to suppress legitimate efforts to change discriminatory practices. It is far more constructive to attack the conditions and grievances which the Communist Party can exploit and to develop the national consensus and its reflection in mass popular parties which provide the best insurance against the rise of totalitarian-minded groups. At this point, therefore, it is important to consider the development of the mass party in democratic states.

The Rise of the Mass Party

Although political parties are now recognized as the dynamic of the democratic political process and the chief means whereby popular control can be exercised, this has not always been the case. When organized political parties first arose in Great Britain and on the Continent, they were aristocratic cliques or factions seeking to protect the interests of their particular group against monarchical demands, although, especially in Britain, some of their members had a strong sense of public responsibility. With the rise of the bourgeoisie came what Max Weber called "parties of notables," informal associations built around those persons who actually held parliamentary seats. This stage of party development was characteristic of British parties after the Parliamentary Reform of 1832, of the political groups in the German Parliament of 1848, of parties in pre-Fascist Italy, and among the center and rightist groups under the French Third Republic. There is also a parallel in the efforts of the Federalists in the early days of American independence to preserve the monopoly of political office by persons of property and position.

But this stage of party development has virtually ceased to exist. Its place has been taken by the mass party, as evident in the United States and Great Britain as it is in India or Mexico. The mass party is the natural outcome of universal suffrage and of the need to appeal broadly to different groups in the community. In contrast to the earlier party of notables, the mass party not only attempts to appeal to all groups in the community, but also tends to be highly organized on a national level (at least at election time), with increasing power resting in the hands of party functionaries. At the same time, it is the mass party's representatives in parliament who are ultimately responsible for policies, and they rarely abdicate this responsibility to the professional party organization which did so much to put them in office.

Political parties in the older democracies, and especially the older, more conservative parties, reached the stage of mass appeal and professional country-wide organization only by degrees. In the United States, for instance, parties are still organized largely at the state and local (county) level and become national organizations only at four-year intervals. This has been the reason why a so far exceptional attempt on the part of an ideologically minded faction of a major American party—the "conservative" or Goldwater wing of the Republican Party —failed in its attempt in 1964 to establish central and continued control over the entire party. What happened was that, having acquired control at the party's nominating convention, the Goldwaterites lost it again after the defeat of their Presidential candidate, and decentralized controls were reassumed by various sectional party leaders, such as state governors and certain leading Republican senators and congressmen.

In Germany, a country of much higher centralization of party life and party organization, the "bourgeois" parties, such as the Christian Democratic Party (CDU), still have not attained the degree of cohesion which has long been characteristic of the Social Democrats (SPD), as is attested to by the much lower percentage of the CDU's formal membership, not to mention the greater interest in party affairs taken by the average member of the SPD. Even in Great Britain, the Conservative Party only slowly adopted the high degree of organization it possesses today, and then largely to counter the impact of Labour, whose popular appeal and disciplined cohesion were its strongest weapons against the entrenched economic strength of the two older British parties. In both Australia and New Zealand, the more conservative parties—the Liberal Party in Australia and the National Party in New Zealand—were even slower to develop a high degree of organization or a popular mass appeal, doing so only as late as the elections of 1949, at which time both these parties ousted Labour administrations from office. In contrast, neither the Liberal nor the Conservative Party in Canada is as yet highly organized, except at election time. There as in the United States, political parties tend to be great holding companies, incorporating conflicting interests and maintaining their cohesion through the imprint of characteristic attitudes—the Canadian Liberals and the American Democratic Party being innovators and social-minded, whereas the concern of the Canadian Progressive Conservative Party and of the American Republicans is directed more toward the balanced budget—as well as through the struggle for political power. Under these circumstances, there is less need to develop highly organized national structures such as are characteristic of present-day British parties or socialist parties on the Continent.

A distinction can be made, in fact, between what is called a party of individual representation and a party of social integration. The former is concerned chiefly with political functions, as is still largely true in Canada and the United States, and even with these on a limited scale. Although the appeal is directed at the whole community, it is generally made only at election time. Moreover, the representative, once chosen, feels free to make his own judgments on issues, to the detriment of party solidarity—a particular characteristic of Southern Democrats in the United States, but by no means restricted to them. The party of social integration, on the other hand, demands much more of its members in terms of financial support, of continuous concern with issues, and of a coordinated view of life. Its representatives are under stricter party discipline. In this respect, the election system, as we have seen, has a bearing: the list system of PR makes the individual representative more dependent on the party leadership than do other systems. In addition, the constitutional system itself has an impact, for where the threat of dissolution of parliament hangs constantly over its members, as in Britain, at least those belonging to the majority party will think twice before kicking against policies of their leaders (i.e., the cabinet), whereas the absence of this possibility, as was true formerly in France, and remains true in the United States, contributes to the feeling of independence the individual deputy enjoys.

Socialist parties, with their coherent world-view and corresponding attitudes and policies, have been among the earliest to belong to the integrated type. But as governments most everywhere assume more responsibilities for economic and social life, there is a natural trend toward turning any party of representation into one of social integration. As long as such a party neither aims at the total conquest of power nor operates in so exclusive a fashion as to imperil the basic consensus on which all stable democratic societies must rest, this process does not threaten but complements the mass democracy of the twentieth century.

This danger of imperiling basic consensus is illustrated, however, by one of the most distinctive of modern mass parties, the Nationalist Party in South Africa. Even in the nineteenth century, the Afrikaner people were organizing themselves into groups with suggestive names like Het Volk (The People). Within two years of the coming into being of the South African Parliament in 1910, the first Afrikaner Nationalist Party was formed. In 1948, when the contemporary Nationalist Party acquired sole governing power in the Union for the first time, it had become as completely the political representative of the great mass of the Afrikaner people as the Dutch Reformed Church was their religious vehicle. Moreover, the Nationalists have developed a highly organized party machinery which uses professionals to direct the constant activities of a large body of volunteer workers. Thus the strength of the party rests on two virtually unassailable pillars: a high degree of organization, and a fervent sense of separate identity of the Afrikaner people, which can be constantly reinforced by appeals to their genuine fear of cultural as well as physical submergence by numerically dominant nonwhites.

The Nationalists represent an unusually close identification of a political party with a particular racial group. So close an identification, whether with a particular racial or social group, may well mean, as we shall see later, that the representative aspect of a political party outweighs the responsible aspect. In other words, a political party, like a political representative, has two functions: it must heed the wishes and interests of those who have put it into office as well as of the formal membership of its group, but it ought also to have regard for the interests of the whole country. For either political programs or political leadership to be limited to the interests of a single group may tend to split or to distort the character of the community if that party acquires political power.

Two-Party Versus Multiparty Systems

The sharp and fundamental distinction between political party systems, as we have seen, is between those in totalitarian and those in democratic countries. But there are also very considerable differences between characteristically two-party systems such as we find in Great Britain, the United States, Canada, Australia, New Zealand, and South Africa, and the multiparty systems of Continental Europe. Most of the traditional two-party systems also include one or more smaller parties, as Great Britain, for example, includes the Liberal Party; Canada, the New Democratic Party (NDP) and the Social Credit Party; South Africa, the Liberal and, since 1959, the Progressive Party. But the essential contest is between two parties only. The third, or the third and fourth parties, may secure a limited number of seats, but not enough to become the official opposition. Thus the election takes on the characteristic of a contest between two major opposing forces, and the voter may cast his vote for a political group which is certain either to form the government or to become its relentless critic.

In multiparty systems, however, the voter can never be sure whether the party for which he votes is going to form the central part of a governing coalition or not. The process of compromise which goes on within a given political party in the average two-party system (and particularly in one like the American or Canadian system, which finds business, labor, and farmers in both major parties) in a multiparty system is transferred to the floor of the assembly, or to the chambers where party leaders meet to hammer out the composition and program of a coalition government. This often enhances the authority of the assembly and the independence of the ordinary member of that body. Unless his party is a strongly disciplined one, like the French Communist or even the French Socialist Party, the member has a chance to exercise his own discretion about policies, and particularly about who should be the premier, in a way which is completely foreign to two-party systems. The penalty (and it is a big one) is that governments tend to rise and fall with dismaying regularity, as they did in both the Third and the postwar Fourth Republics in France. Moreover, it is difficult to secure continuity of policies except through the action of the administration, which is thereby enhanced in power. In addition, this system has the great disadvantage of usually not presenting the voter with a choice of leaders who, as chiefs of a party gaining the majority, will be sure to become the head of government, since in a multiparty system the postelection negotiations of the parties determine which one will present the prime minister. That party may even turn out to be one of the smaller entities forming the government coalition.

It is commonly said that what determines whether there is a two-party or multiparty system is the degree of unity of the particular community. Multiparty systems obviously reflect divisions within the community—in social structure, economic interest, racial composition, or ideological preference. But that naturally disparate groups can be held together by a strong personality and the overriding importance of a few major issues has been proved by the experience of West Germany. Much the same task as Dr. Adenauer performed in West Germany was carried out successfully by Pandit Nehru in India during its transition to a linguistic basis for federalism. But when cleavages go deep in a country and are felt intensely, only exceptional circumstances and leadership—like that of General Charles de Gaulle in France—are capable of bridging them. Moreover, unless new allegiances develop which are stronger than the divisive factors, multiparty divisions tend to take hold again and once more seriously to handicap effective government should that leadership be removed.

But two-party systems have their own problems. This is true especially where, as in Great Britain, Australia, and New Zealand, parties divide on a class basis, or where, as in Canada and South Africa, there are racial divisions to be bridged. Before 1924, some political observers even believed that Labour would never be able to achieve office in Great Britain without a violent reaction, since they felt that the propertied groups in the community would feel too threatened by its objectives to allow such a program to be imposed peacefully. That this did not happen reflects a major degree of agreement on fundamentals between the Labour Party and the other parties in Great Britain, and in New Zealand and Australia as well (where Labour achieved national office as early as 1908). It also reflects the fact that the programs introduced by Labour, when it came into office in those countries, corresponded to the social conscience or, in the latter two countries, to the equalitarian views, of the community at that particular moment.

This explains two phenomena: why Labour was able when it first came to power to carry through its program so quickly and without difficulty in all three of these countries, and why in each case the Labour Party tended to lose its momentum and appeal so soon after instituting its reforms. What seems obvious is that once a simple reformist program has been carried through by a labor party, it confronts the much more difficult issue of whether to introduce more than palliatives to curb the inequities and dislocations inherent in capitalism. It confronts the dilemma, in other words, of whether to be representative of its own particularism or whether to be responsible to the basic ways of action of the whole community. If it drastically attacks the prevailing economic modes, it risks alienating its own right wing and even more the middle-class groups on which it depends for electoral success. If not, it alienates its own more radical members and loses its drive. Thereafter, paradoxically, its greatest appeal to the electorate may well be that it can do better administratively than its conservative opponents —who in the meantime have adopted the more attractive parts of labor's program. The end result in these cases is that the consensus of the community is strengthened, while effective government is maintained.

This trend toward moderation has been characteristic of other labor parties too, in particular the originally more radical and dogmatic socialist parties of the Continent. Many of these parties have played an effective role in coalition governments, and where, as in West Germany, they may become the leading government party, there are few who are still afraid that their policies would deviate from the mildly reformist pattern set by their more recent party programs (such as the Godesberg program of the West German SPD). This entire development reflects the entrance of formerly proletarian and underprivileged classes (such as the industrial workers) into the "affluent society" of the industrially advanced nations. In the less advanced countries there is less of a basis for this process. Even in the developed nations there are still found "pockets of poverty" and neglected groups which may look for more radical representation of their interests if reformist parties overlook them.

That the process of consensus formation on the basis of moderation can take place even where racial rather than social and economic divisions are concerned is proved by the experience of Canada. In that country—with the exception of the split over conscription between English- and French-Canadians during World War I—the national-party system has hardly ever reflected racial divisions. The French-speaking minority is always represented within the governing party (in the long Liberal reign from 1935 to 1957, virtually all of Quebec's representatives were on the government side), and this ensures consideration of its distinctive point of view. The fact that the English- and French-speaking population work together in the same party, or parties, also aids mutual understanding and the building of consensus, though strains appear sharply from time to time.

In South Africa, in contrast, the United Party, which then combined practically all the English-speaking population with a small percentage of Afrikaans-speaking South Africans under an Afrikaner leader, was dispossessed of political power in 1948 by the Nationalist Party with its exclusively Afrikaner membership and leadership. The result was at first a noticeable sharpening of racial feeling between the two groups. Largely because all white people in the Union are conscious of their need to retain something of a common front against the non-whites, who outnumber them four to one, the division between Afrikaners and English-speaking people did not become dangerous, and indeed seems largely bridged by an increasing sense of danger to the last major white resident minority on the continent. This experience suggests that under normal circumstances, a political party composed of one racial (or any other exclusivist) group tends to accentuate divisions in a country, and thus either to lessen the nation's consensus or, if a particular crisis develops, to result in an externally or self-imposed new pattern of conformity. Thus, somewhat paradoxically, the two-party system can also reflect a situation in which a reluctant minority increasingly conforms to the will of a parliamentary majority instead of performing the functions of criticism and of presenting alternative programs which are the essence of the constructive role of the parliamentary opposition.

Party Financing

With the rise of the mass party, the question of who pays for party work and party offices, party employees, and, in particular, campaign and other election expenditures has become an ever more urgent one. At the time of party "notables," persons of independent means could still finance their own campaigns. While this fact, of course, favored wealth, it was so to speak self-contained wealth, and the successful candidate, on the whole, was not beholden to persons or groups that backed him financially in expectation of reward. Today, the financing of a mass party and its election campaign requires vast amounts of money, which, in principle, can be secured in two ways: by numerous generally small contributions of party members and voters, or by fewer but larger subsidies from special-interest groups, such as business enterprises, agricultural organizations, and trade unions. In our day, especially since the organization of nationwide campaigns (which include arrangements for television and radio appearances of candidates), electioneering has become a fine and expensive art. Thus the question of from whom and how a party secures its major support can be decisive not only for its subsequent attitudes and policies, but for its very success at the polls.

It is here that the functioning of the democratic process meets a vital test. If equality of opportunity in the political field is to have more than a mere formal meaning, it must imply at least some degree of equality in the means essential for political success. But this ideal is far from being realized in most democratic systems. It is well known that in the United States, for example, the Republican Party is usually favored over the Democratic Party in regard to availability of campaign funds (in the 1956 election the proportion was roughly by 2:1).

The most striking recent example of such "inequality in financial opportunity" is perhaps furnished by West Germany, where industry has established so-called promoters' associations, which assess the individual enterprises according to their payroll and distribute the levies among the government parties (with the chief portion, of course, going to the CDU). The Social Democrats, compelled to rely on membership dues and similar small contributions, have only much smaller amounts at their disposal. To avoid open scandal, therefore, the three major parties prior to the 1965 election agreed to limit their campaign expenditures to approximately equal amounts. At the same time, it was decided to lessen their dependence on private contributions by subsidizing them through annual stipends from public funds. This process, however, may make the parties appear even more like "official" institutions than they already are.

In Great Britain, a system more effective in limiting campaign expenditures than that in the United States has prevented the extremes of plutocratic abuses. The law specifies financial limits during the election period and restricts "treating" and other defined forms of influence. In Canada, big business commonly contributes to both major parties, though a higher percentage is given to the one in power. But the problem is a serious one, and unless and until they solve it, democracies will continue to be exposed to charges that behind their egalitarian façade, rich men or powerful pressure groups are in control.

The Mass Party in the Newer States

While mass parties evolved slowly in the older democratic states, they have been a characteristic of the newer states from the beginning. Where a nationalistic movement is struggling to bring a country to independence, its natural focus is in a mass party which unites virtually all elements in the country in a common demand for transfer of power. As independence comes close or is achieved, strains may develop, however, which split the mass party into communal or tribally oriented groups. In British India, for example, the Moslem League refused to work with the Congress Party with its largely Hindu support and secular philosophy, and the ultimate result was that the sub-continent had to be partitioned between Pakistan and India.

In the Gold Coast (subsequently Ghana), middle-class and tribally oriented groups combined against the standard-bearer of nationalism, Kwame Nkrumah's Convention Peoples Party (commonly known as the CPP), in the years immediately pre-ceding independence. In an effort to satisfy them, the British insisted that Ghana should establish regional assemblies to share power with the national legislature, but these were voted out of existence almost as soon as they came into being, and Ghana has become a one-party state. A similar process took place in Kenya, where a single comprehensive party now in-cludes members of the pre-independence rival parties KANU and KADU.

Is there no middle way between a single dominant mass party in newly developing states and anarchy threatening to lead to army or dictatorial rule? Possibly not. The problem of emerging Asian and African states still is more a social than a political one: It is the need to build a strong enough sense of unity in the country so that criticism and diversity do not seem like treason. Wherever there is a serious split in the nationalist movement prior to independence, the group in opposition is almost inevitably labeled treasonable. If this split persists after independence, either force or a long period of stability are needed to heal it. The kind of divisions which are welcomed in well-established democracies may shatter the fragile chances of national unity in ethnically diverse societies.

One-Party Democracy

Though most independent African states no longer have a two-party or multiparty political system, their leaders commonly assert that they are neither dictatorships nor totalitarian but "one-party democracies." The justification for this designation is twofold: that a formal opposition party would only accentuate existing differences and divisions, whereas these potential sources of strain can be given expression and can be reconciled within the single political group; and that there is no place for the traditional parliamentary battle when existing skill and experience are all too limited and all energies and talents are needed to advance national development.

Is this democracy? We have been accustomed to say that one-party rule and dictatorship are virtually synonymous. But even in the early days of the United States, there was only one party, the Federalists, until Jefferson stimulated the rise of what was little more than a personal political movement. When the Federalist Party collapsed, the country was left for some time without an organized alternative to Jefferson's Republican Party. Yet in the long run, of course, the American two-party system emerged. While it is natural for the older Western democracies to look for two-party systems and ultimate alternation of office in the new countries, this process requires experience, a substantial pool of talent, and a fairly firm social structure. It exists to some degree in Nigeria, where it is encouraged by the very diversity of the regions, but even in that populous country coalition governments have been the practice. Moreover, Chief Awolowo and his associates in the Action Party were repressed after being accused of threatening the national government with violence when their chances of peaceful accession to power seemed increasingly remote. For most of the new countries, the touchstone of democracy will not be the number of parties engaged in debate in the parliamentary arena, but the right to express open criticism and the maintenance of the rule of law. If these two essentials exist, the future may well see the evolution of what we consider the more orthodox structure of democratic government.

What we have called "one-party democracy" differs basically, it must be emphasized, from the one-party totalitarianism of the Soviet Union itself or other Communist-controlled countries. In the first instance the presence of only one party is not a dogma but an expedient. The objective is to mobilize the people voluntarily to work for the vastly important objective of national development. In this sense, "one-party democracy" has some similarities to the unity most Western democratic states established while they were fighting what President Franklin D. Roosevelt called "the war of survival"—World War II.

The possibilities of criticism within the one-party democracy provide in themselves a type of opposition that should not be underestimated. The mass parties in the newly developing countries are far from monolithic. It is far more difficult to identify and classify the kind of opposition which operates within these African countries than it would be if the opposition were organized as a separate party, but forthright criticism by backbenchers in both Kenya and Tanzania of governmental slowness in implementing pledges of East African Federation makes it clear that such opposition can both exist and be vocal. In fact, it is possible for something very close to the interplay of government and opposition in mature democracies to take place within the single party of the new states, but only, of course, if opportunities for criticism are not stifled.

Army Rule

In a striking number of cases, new parliamentary democracies which failed to work efficiently have come under army rule. In the Sudan, in Pakistan, in Burma, in Egypt, in Iraq, and in Turkey, military leaders have run or are running the civilian machinery of government. In part, these situations have been the result of internal or external threats, in particular by Communists, or, in the Near Eastern region, by Nasser as self-appointed leader of Arab unification, but more especially they arose out of parliamentary weaknesses and crises. Western democracies usually look with disquiet at the establishment of military dictatorships, and this is historically justified in view of their own experience with the phenomenon known as "Bonapartism." But in the new countries, the army sometimes possesses more liberal-minded and well-trained people than are found among the politicians. In these developing countries, authoritarianism, as we have seen, can perform the function of an "educational dictatorship" which is progressive because it aims at modernization and the requisite reforms. If so, or if army rule become oppressive, it may eventually give way, as in the Sudan in 1964–65, to more liberal and democratic processes.

Much depends, of course, on the program of the army leader who comes into power. There is a similarity between the forms of local representation adopted in Egypt and in Pakistan respectively under Colonel Nasser and General Mohammed Ayub Khan, yet there is a great difference in the methods they have used in attempting to shape their respective societies. As far as institutions are concerned, both have established directly elected village and town councils as the lowest level of representation, arguing with some justification that illiterate peasants can choose better from among those they know personally than between rival parties. On this base, a pyramidal system of indirect election from one level to the next has been erected.

This attempt to substitute consensus in a representative system for party government is said to avoid unnatural divisions and to reflect the so-called traditional "village democracy" of which Asian and African leaders sometimes boast. But while Ayub Khan concentrated on land reform and on tackling local problems, Nasser embarked on a radical reorganization of the economy, using nationalization as a major instrument. As a consequence, the village-oriented social and economic program on which Ayub Khan has embarked has a closer relationship to the local councils which form the basis of representation than is true in Egypt.

It is open to question, however, whether in the long run any representative system based on the hypothesis that decisions must be the result of general consensus or agreement can avoid the danger of crushing opportunities for the expression of independent thinking. "Village democracy" arose out of circumstances providing limited alternatives, or even an absence of alternatives. It reflects narrow horizons, perhaps bounded by the physical limits of the village itself. As, with modernization, the village becomes part of a much larger entity with a wide range of alternatives and is affected by swift-moving social and economic change, the strain on the traditional consensus becomes great. There is an arithmetic, if not a geometric, relationship between the number of possible alternatives of action and the speed of social and economic change. The opportunity to argue out these alternatives, at least in the interest of understandability and of a check on possible arbitrariness, may also produce a more solidly knit community than institutions which are directed toward glossing over such differences of view.

It is not only under army rule that such issues arise. The one-party democracies of which we have spoken are also eager to enjoy a consensus in regard to their policies. Since popular support is necessarily one of the criteria by which we judge the degree of democracy of such regimes, it is particularly important to be alert to the degree to which that support is secured through techniques which muffle opposition or genuinely arises as the result of the interaction of alternatives.

Army rule in some areas other than the United Arab Republic and Pakistan has been replaced by largely democratic structures. Turkey was initially transformed from a traditionalist Islamic state to a secular republic and acquired stability, economic growth, and a secure international position under the authoritarian rule of its great leader Kemal Pasha, better known as Atatürk. In 1945, President Inönü somewhat precipitously introduced a multiparty Western-style parliamentary system with popular elections. In 1960, the Menderes regime was overthrown by an army group, but parliamentary government has since been re-established under Inönü. In the Sudan, there was little evidence that army rule improved what was admittedly an unstable situation under the regime of parties. A series of army coups in the first months of the military regime resulted in broadening the base of authority, but ultimately led to bloodshed, while repression of the Southern Sudan was, if anything, intensified. If army rule thus provided a fragile base for the re-establishment of democratic government in 1965, it was also an experience which few Sudanese seek to repeat. Thus the character of the army leadership and, perhaps still more important, the way it approaches the kinds of division existing within the country, determine the impact of army rule and the degree to which it provides a foundation for a more democratic system.

Postwar experience of types of rule in newly independent countries includes a wide variety of means to combine effective and, hopefully, public-spirited administration with economic development and encouragement of national cohesion. Some leaders have maintained that authoritarianism is essential for the maintenance of stability and for demanding the sacrifices necessary for development; others claim that parliamentary institutions provide the framework within which leadership can be combined with public airing of issues and restraint on arbitrary action. Neither view is necessarily valid for a particular situation. It is important to recognize that the operation of parliamentary institutions in such a way as to provide effective and yet responsible government requires a considerable degree of experience and of restraint. The Belgians obviously gave such institutions little or no chance of success in the Congo by bestowing them only a few weeks before the territory achieved independence on June 30, 1960. Yet among the former British and former French territories of Africa, some—like Nigeria, Senegal, Uganda, and Zambia—have not been unsuccessful in handling parliamentary institutions, which provide legitimacy and a known method of succession in a way which authoritarian regimes cannot duplicate. At their best, they also provide for the ventilation of issues, so that feelings are not bottled up until they reach the explosion point.

What the experience of army rule and one-party democracies may indicate is that the urge to express opposing views, and the corrective balance wheel to authoritarianism of such outlets, may be found in many more places than traditional political analysis has suggested. Within a democratic one-party system, the opposition may make itself felt through trade unions or youth or women's groups; it may be provided by the army acting in a nonpolitical but somewhat censorlike role; or by the civil service acting in the same nonpartisan fashion and allowed by the ruling politicians to do so. As long as this is the case, the stifling effects of authoritarianism are lessened, the opportunities for social growth are enhanced, and cohesion and stability are combined with criticism. In comparison with this somewhat sensitive balance, unresponsive dictatorship—whether veiled in parliamentary forms or on forms built on a system of village councils, or exercised openly to the accompaniment of inflammatory nationalist propaganda—tends to an enforced uniformity within which opposition can express itself only through violence.

LEGISLATURES

The end result of the activity of political parties is to place their candidates in the elected, representative assembly (or assemblies) still usually referred to as a legislature. Under the presidential system, the chief executive is likewise the product of direct party contest and election; thus, in the United States, not only the two houses of the legislature but also the Presidency are based on direct popular support. In the parliamentary system, on the other hand, the executive issues technically from the legislature and, in this way, only indirectly from party contest and popular vote. But especially where there is a two-party system, the electoral contest, although ostensibly only concerned with the election of members of the legislature, tends more and more to be tantamount to a plebiscite on the leadership of the government. This has been traditionally the situation in Great Britain, and more recently it has become so in West Germany.

In a few countries, for example, Norway or Israel, the legislature is organized as a unicameral body. Commonly, however, a legislature is composed of two houses. The reasons for having a second chamber vary. Occasionally, it is a remnant of the predemocratic past, providing for the representation of nobility and similar groups. Thus, in Great Britain, the House of Lords—by now shorn of most of its formerly vital functions—in part still rests on hereditary succession, though in part on appointment. In other instances, the objective is to provide a chamber that is more conservative (in the general, not necessarily the party-political sense of the word) than the popularly elected house, a result usually achieved through an indirect method of selection by persons themselves elected to other bodies. This process, used in France and South Africa, for example, tends not only to make the second chamber more conservative but also weaker than the popularly elected one. This is true, of course, also for Great Britain (and Canada, where senators are appointed), because in a democratic period people consider those popularly and directly elected to be their most "legitimate" representatives. Thus the second chamber tends to recede into the background and to be useful (where it is not hampering) as a place for consideration of issues which the popularly elected chamber does not have time adequately to explore, or to provide another point of view.

The most frequent reason, however, for the existence of two houses is a federal structure of government. In federally organized countries, as we have seen, the second chamber, representing the member units, can be organized in different ways. In some countries, like Germany, it is not elected but consists of representatives of the governments of the member states, thus only indirectly reflecting the party constellations in these units. In others, like Australia, Switzerland, and the United States, its members are popularly elected but from differently demarcated constituencies. In either case, these second chambers may be of equal importance and on an equal footing with the one selected through the over-all national elections.

Where, as in the Presidential-Congressional system of the United States, direct election underpins the power and prestige of both legislative chambers and of the chief executive as well, there is a natural basis for the system of checks and balances, which can operate despite the links among all three created by political parties. But in a parliamentary system, where the executive is not separate from the legislature, there is an almost irresistible tendency toward the dominance of either the cabinet or the lower chamber, even if both legislative bodies are elective. Few chambers were so buttressed in power as the French National Assembly under the Fourth Republic; under the Fifth Republic it has become a mere shadow of its former self as the President and Cabinet have become dominant. The British House of Commons occupies a position midway between the French National Assembly of the Fourth and Fifth Republics—a body of distinction but under the control of the Cabinet.

There was a time when democratic theory (originating in Rousseauian and Jacobin ideas) was inclined to look upon an assembly, which directly issued from popular elections and thus immediately reflected the "will of the people," as *the* supreme organ of government, in principle entitled to conduct all the affairs of state, and in particular to be in full and complete charge of lawmaking. At certain times and in certain countries, the legislature was more prominent than it usually is today. But the idea that "representative" government requires a parliamentary body with the above-mentioned all-encompassing powers was wrong in any event. Representative government in this sense could not exist even under the best of circumstances. To expect any large and varied group of average, inexpert representatives to frame the laws of a complex society and to coordinate a government's far-flung activities is to impose a burden which no representative assembly can be expected to bear.

What a well-organized assembly can do—and do well—is to analyze, criticize, and judge the policies and proposals of the government; to voice the desires and anxieties of the mass of the citizens; to protect their liberties against any abuse of power by the government; to educate public opinion through its debates; and finally—as the term legislature implies—to participate in the process of lawmaking to the extent this is still possible in an area that relies increasingly on the expert and the administrator. In some ways, the legislature is particularly suited to these tasks. If its members lack the expert knowledge necessary to frame technical legislation, they possess a different kind of knowledge, which the experts themselves are not likely to have: the legislators, taken in the mass, represent a range of experience in terms of class and geographical origin and in intimate knowledge of their constituents which makes them exceptionally good judges of public opinion and of the acceptability and workability of laws.

In the Soviet Union, as one would expect, the aim is different; the Supreme Soviet is, in practice, expected to perform only a few of these functions. Great care is taken to make that body as representative as possible in a vocational and a national sense; but the purpose is not to permit these representatives to oversee and criticize the government, but rather to permit the government to educate them (and through them the people) in its purposes and policies. Thus there is no criticism of the government's policies, and what criticism there is of administration stops short of the leaders of the Communist Party and, presumably, is permitted only with their approval.

The same applies to the parliaments of the Soviet orbit countries, whatever the method by which they are elected, and even if, as in the German Democratic Republic, other parties are represented together with "mass organizations." Since these organizations as well as the non-Communist parties are under the control of the "state party," they are dependent on Communist leadership and exist chiefly for decorative or propagandistic purposes. One possible exception is the Polish Seym, where one parliamentary group (a Catholic one) has been allowed to voice occasional criticism, or even opposition.

When one turns to the Western democracies, it is evident that both the British Parliament and the French National Assembly under the Fourth Republic performed certain (though not the same) functions admirably. As protector of individual liberties against any abuse of governmental power, the House of Commons is unexcelled. As educator of the public on important issues, its well-organized and -publicized debates are remarkably effective. As critic of proposed legislation, the Opposition, at its best, is highly effective. The chief criticisms to which Parliament is subjected concern its lack of expertness (which detracts both from the cogency of its legislative criticism and from its ability to supervise the increasingly complex activities of the civil service), the rigor of party discipline (which allegedly destroys the independence and initiative of the private member), the failure to reflect with exactness the strength and varieties of political opinion in Great Britain, and subserviency to the Cabinet.

In postwar France of the Fourth Republic, in contrast, the National Assembly more accurately reflected the diversity of opinion and the popular vote, and the system of specialized committees provided members with greater knowledge and rendered them more fit to cope with the technicalities of modern legislation and administration. Although there were complaints of excessive discipline among some of the parties of the left, the deputies in the center and on the right enjoyed a large degree of independence. And, unlike the British Parliament, in normal times the French National Assembly demonstrated its control over the Cabinet by rejecting or making serious modifications in its proposals. In spite of these merits, however, few people would consider the Fourth Republic's National Assembly a model democratic legislative body. The inability of the different party groups to agree upon an effective legislative program and to support a stable government, the violent and undisciplined debate and the uncompromising hostility between different political interests, the eagerness of certain partisans on the extreme left and the extreme right to discredit parliamentary democracy by making effective action impossible, all helped to give currency to the popular picture of the legislature as a forum of bickering, irresponsible, special interests. This tended to make men more amenable to follow a leader who promised political stability and the placing of the national interest above party interests, and thus paved the way for De Gaulle's Fifth Republic.

Nor does the German Parliament, whether under the Weimar or the present Bonn Republic, offer a much more reassuring picture. Traditionally, the German executive was more independent of parliament and parties than was the French, with the result that in Germany, parliamentary control of the executive was often ineffectual. The ensuing conflicts between popular forces and an authoritarian-minded governing elite discredited democratic procedures and representative institutions time and again, thereby opening the way for the executive to assume uncontrolled power.

Today, while it would be exaggerated to suggest that the executive is unrestricted politically, it is true that it does control the procedure of law-making in large measure. The expert ministerial bureaucracy drafts and initiates almost all important bills, adapts them to local and state needs through the second chamber (another bureaucratically composed body), steers them through Bundestag committees by its presence and powerful influence there, and subsequently, of course, oversees their administration. In the course of this process, Parliament has made little use so far of the possibilities of surveillance and criticism which the Constitution and its own standing orders provide. Where, more recently, some lively criticism of executive abuses and arbitrariness has been voiced in West Germany, it has been the press and other voices of general public opinion that have taken the lead, rather than the Bundestag. This was the case, as we have seen, in the notorious *Spiegel* affair, as a result of which Chancellor Adenauer was compelled to drop one of his closest aides, Defense Minister Franz Josef Strauss.

A similar erosion, or lack of use of parliamentary power and influence, constantly threatens the new or semidemocratic countries. One of the characteristics of the mass party, as we have seen, is its dependence on its leader or leaders; the very effort of nation-making and of attempting to assert a new importance in international affairs encourages use of the legislative body as a sounding board rather than as a critic. The lack of administrative training and experience which handicaps legislators everywhere is most obvious in capitals like Lagos, Colombo, Nairobi, and Mexico City. This is not to say that the legislators in these and similar countries do not work hard (they do), but rather that the combination of responsiveness to public attitudes and needs and of detailed supervision of executive action which is the mark of the better members of mature legislatures requires a sense of judgment and of overriding loyalty to the state uncommonly difficult to acquire in countries only gradually emerging from caste, or tribal, or family-oriented social structures.

Some of the difficulties resulting from allegiance to local rather than national interests are illustrated even in the American Congress. A congressman's party affiliation may be less important than the area from which he comes or the special interests in his constituency. This can lead not only to "logrolling" in the passage of legislation, but also to somewhat erratic and even arbitrary supervision of executive action, as has been true of the use of certain investigating committees. Moreover, the power of congressional committees, especially in finance, seriously limits the ability of the executive to present a coordinated program. That none of these factors provides any insuperable obstacles either to efficient or to responsible government is obvious from the operations of American government; but similar sectionalism in less unified and mature countries can all too easily lead either to a frustrated administration or, as its corollary, authoritarianism.

What emerges from these comparisons is the fact that some of the frequently criticized defects of the British Parliament (and also of the Canadian and Australian Parliaments) are responsible, at least in part, for their freedom from the confusion, irresponsibility, and deadlock with which the French legislature of the Fourth Republic was rightly charged, or the lack of effectiveness of parliamentary action found in Germany and even more in most of the newer countries. If the system of representation is far from perfect in Great Britain, both in reflecting shades of political opinion and in commonly exaggerating the majority of the larger party, these very distortions usually provide a stronger and more stable government capable of introducing a comprehensive program and of carrying it through. Party discipline not only reinforces this stability, but contributes to the responsibility and the educational value of the British system. It is true that Sweden with its multiparty system also provides stable and clear-cut government; but this is largely because the party combinations which furnish the executive do not fluctuate sharply (as was the case in France's Fourth Republic) and also because its party groups provide fairly clear-cut alternatives at election time. But if party members fail to vote as a unit, it is impossible for the voters either to understand or to judge the party's position; and there is no assurance that a party, once elected, will have either the desire or the power to carry out its promises to the voters. It is at this point, in particular, that the ultimate responsibility to the voters implicit in representative government links up with the legislature's role of supervision and restraint on the executive.

A word should perhaps be said about the problems of the technical organization of parliament in the twentieth century and the personal status of its members, for these questions are not without influence on politics and the functioning of government. While the more relaxed pace of life in previous centuries permitted a representative body to proceed leisurely and intermittently, leaving its members to their own devices as far as income and information were concerned, and organized according to archaic rules that often reflected colorful customs but were hardly conducive to a smooth transaction of business, the conditions and demands of the technological age would seem to require modernization here as elsewhere. But few parliaments are set up to fit the requirements of the century. Calendars are chronically congested in all modern parliaments. Frequently, those with vested interests in inaction or in stalling action when legislation threatens their own or their "customers'" status or interests, prevent organizational reforms and change of rules, as has been most apparent in American legislatures, especially in the Congress itself. And while Congress, at least, has recently been given the technical assistance of ample staffs and an effective legislative reference service in preparing or coordinating legislative proposals, and now also provides adequate pay for its members, the state legislatures in the United States for the most part still meet only intermittently, provide too little pay for their members, and virtually no assistance in their work. The West German Bundestag likewise does not provide its members with expert reference services. And British adherence to the ancient pageantry of Parliament, which is copied by many a new legislature of formerly British countries, while perhaps useful as an "integrating" part of the constitution, and thus of the nation, has meant that there are not even enough seats in the House to accommodate all its members, let alone adequate provision of assistance.

For a variety of reasons, the weight of government in this century has shifted from the legislature to the executive, and this development cannot fail to affect the image of parliament in the eyes of the public. Even as a forum for the executive leadership's pronouncements on important issues parliament has declined. A chief executive, returning from an important meeting abroad, will be besieged for information by the representatives of the publicity "media" as soon as his jet plane touches down at the airport. And more likely than not he will feel that he cannot withhold important facts until the next meeting of parliament, and thus its members will, in this situation, be relegated to the position of the general public, and their debate (if any) will take second place to that being carried on in the press and elsewhere.

Yet it is clear that legislatures can yet fulfill important, and indeed vital, functions, provided that their members are alert to public tasks and to the interests of the whole community and avoid being mere mouthpieces either of their parties and "party lines" or else of special interests chiefly concerned with how the big pie is cut. In particular, the members of the opposition must know how to provide meaningful alternatives even where there is agreement on fundamentals. Nothing endangers the role of a modern parliament more than the transformation of an opposition into a mere "me-too" group appeased by the majority and the executive with a few crumbs of influence and patronage.

VI

POLITICAL LEADERSHIP
AND ADMINISTRATION

Throughout our discussions of how to keep government responsible, we have referred to the importance of political leadership. With the spectacular growth in the functions of government which has taken place in every advanced country, the power of the executive has grown proportionately. Since, as we have seen, the legislature is not well fitted to perform the tasks of framing and initiating, as distinct from discussing and passing, legislation, or to engage in comprehensive planning, these tasks inevitably fall to the relatively small group of political leaders and top-ranking administrators. Moreover, the leadership function presents in an acute form a basic problem of modern government: how to integrate the numerous and often dissenting groups and interests in our pluralistic societies and at the same time to check overly integrated or concentrated power. Liberal democracy can all too easily develop toward the anarchy of diverse and uncooperating groups, while undemocratic systems tend to develop into authoritarianism and even, ultimately, dictatorship. In both situations, the balance wheel is responsible leadership. Thus, the effort to develop and maintain responsible leadership is the most crucial one for the future of the modern democratic state with its mass electorate and vast multiplicity of tasks.

The Headship of the State:
The Leader "Reigns"

Integration through leadership has a twofold aspect: symbolism and actual authority. Psychologists and sociologists may argue about why it is that every human political organization needs a unifying symbol with or through which it can identify itself as unique and differentiated from every other unit; but the fact is undeniable. The unifying symbol may be impersonal (e.g., the American Constitution in its symbolic character), but more frequently it is embodied in a person. The extreme case of personalized symbolic (and actual) leadership is the totalitarian dictatorship, with its Führer, its Duce, or its "Great Father and Leader," as the Soviet press used to call Stalin. But traditionalist leadership can be as strong as charismatic leadership. Not only divine right but also modern constitutional monarchy is a case in point. It is perhaps no coincidence that fascism as well as Communism, both of which discard traditional symbols for new ones, have been least successful where monarchy as an institution still has strong roots. Thus the British, Dutch, and Swedish crowns, despite their lack of real political power, have proved an antidote to totalitarianism. Moreover, in countries as widely separated as Iran and Thailand, popular monarchs are providing the best hope for stability and for furthering the interests of their people.

This underlines the important function of a head of state, as distinguished from the head of government. Where constitutional monarchies exist, the chief function of the head of state is to symbolize and represent the nation, especially in its foreign relations. Without the monarchy, the Commonwealth of Nations might have disintegrated. Even the Asian and African members who have adopted a republican structure acknowledge the Queen as the symbolic "head" of the Commonwealth, in effect its most visible symbol of unity. Parliamentary-type republican countries, lacking such a "given" head and symbol, face the problem of providing for a dignified headship that can serve as a unifying force. In West Germany, for example, the restraint with which the first President of the new regime, Theodor Heuss, exercised his function, accounts in large measure for the high esteem this office now enjoys. In France, too, the office of President, separated as it was from actual executive power, used to depend for its respect and importance on the person of its holder. Under the Fifth Republic, however, De Gaulle enjoys not only great national prestige, but also vast reserve powers, and, in practice, exercises a major degree of decision-making. Moreover, in an effort to provide his successor with comparable political influence and power, De Gaulle, by dubious constitutional means, pushed through a provision for future direct election of the President. Whether this constitutional change can of itself provide a unifying and directing executive in the face of a multiparty system with no clear majority remains to be seen. Under De Gaulle, a regrouping of parties, plus the presence in the legislature of an unprecedentedly strong party pledged to his policies, have prevented a presidential-legislative confrontation, but it is not out of the realm of possibility in the future.

In the United States, the head of state exercises so much real executive power that both dignity and prestige are never lacking. Though the Constitution is usually considered the primary unifying symbol in the United States, the degree to which the combined head-of-state–chief-executive is the leader of the nation in the people's mind is sharply illustrated when a President dies in office or is struck by sudden illness.

But presidential systems face a serious practical problem: how to relieve the chief executive and political leader, whose tasks are already almost superhuman, from the additional time- and energy-consuming burden involved in his symbolic role. This is why even totalitarian regimes sometimes make use of a person other than the leader for the discharge of symbolic functions, e.g., the King under Italian Fascism, or the Chairman of the Presidium of the Supreme Soviet in the Soviet Union. In the United States, it has been suggested that the Vice-President might assume some of the ceremonial functions of headship. But symbolic leadership, once vested in one office or person, is not easily transferred, nor may its possessor wish it to be transferred. It involves more than legal or constitutional amendments: it involves the mind and the habits of a nation, and where such a division of functions is an innovation it might mean a change in the degree of influence exercised by the incumbent of the particular high office.

THE HEADSHIP OF THE GOVERNMENT: THE LEADER "RULES"

In Democracies

Even leaving aside the symbolic function of political leadership, there remains the bulk of the leader's task, enough to render the job trying under any standards of efficient one-man performance. Such a leader, in a democracy, must lay down the essential lines of policy in every field of domestic and foreign affairs; he must determine basic lines of military policy even in peacetime; he must coordinate the innumerable agencies of what in most modern countries has become the biggest "business establishment"—the executive branch of the government; ordinarily he must lead, and keep together, the majority party (or, in a multiparty system, one of the major parties); he must manage a sometimes hostile, sometimes (in terms of majorities and minorities) unstable, or sometimes (in terms of political discipline) anarchic legislature; he must deal with a vast variety of interest groups and be able to resist their often powerful pressures; he must, to be successful, be alert to, and yet manage, public opinion. He should be a spokesman capable of explaining the problems and policies of government in simple and effective terms. He must ordinarily be able to win an open, competitive election. In a parliamentary democracy he should be able to participate successfully in the give-and-take of debate. He should be able to guide cabinet meetings, reconcile divergent opinions, and preside over the formulation of policy. He should, in addition, be a good administrator, not in the sense of detailed technical competence, but in the ability to oversee the range of administrative activity and to supervise the coordination of policy.

In Dictatorships

In contrast, the task of a totalitarian leader seems simpler. True, his job is still vast in terms of the top decisions to be made. The governmental machine to be organized and coordinated may be even vaster than in democracies, particularly where, as in the Soviet Union or in China, it involves planning and running the economy; as in democracies, it comprises policy-making in the vital fields of foreign affairs and defense. On the other hand, a totalitarian leader does not have to manage a genuine legislature with an opposition or a party with its own will and perhaps conflicting wings. Everything, in this respect, is "coordinated." He does not have to deal with free-ranging, independent pressure groups, though pressures, even dangerous ones, may work behind the scenes. If he must interpret policy to the masses, he does so unimpeded by the interference of a critical opposition or press. His popularity can be created artificially by the officially directed instruments of a manipulated public opinion. Since no opposition is tolerated, he need never win an open election.

Still, it is easy to underestimate the job of a totalitarian dictator. Since in such a regime there is no formal system whereby he accedes to power, the leader must have attained his position through extralegal means (in the democratic sense). As we know from a study of the rise of a Hitler or a Stalin, the means include brute force as well as devious scheming, terroristic propaganda and purges, manipulation of the masses, of important power groups, and of close friends and lieutenants. His rise thus involves a selectivity in which only the fittest—i.e., the toughest—survive. And after having arrived at the top, the leader must maintain himself through similar means, since he is not supported by constitutional legality or traditionalist legitimacy. Moreover, though he does not have to respond to an independent public opinion, he must, through constant interpretation, maintain the "purity" and at least seeming consistency of the doctrine, so as never to leave any doubt about the basic standards—the "line"—of the regime. This, in the case of Soviet leadership, has involved the attempt to coordinate and even direct the doctrinal lines and resulting basic policy approaches of *all* Communist regimes. Failure to maintain this doctrinal leadership, at first in the case of Titoist "revisionism" and subsequently in the face of Maoist "doctrinairism," has accounted for the serious splits that have occurred in the Communist camp, most conspicuously the Soviet-Chinese rift.

The Two Compared

If quick and decisive action is what modern government requires above all else, then, some have argued, it is the authoritarian leaders—proven in cunning and ruthlessness and free from special pressures, constitutional inhibitions, and the need to conciliate genuine opinion—who are far better suited to such conditions than are the democratic leaders. Especially in the vital fields of foreign, defense, and economic policies, concentration of power unhampered by popular or parliamentary controls and free from the danger of periodic change of personnel may appear the better guarantor of efficiency. But such arguments are based on doubtful assumptions. As a matter of fact, the pressures and special influences which openly harry democratic leadership also play on totalitarian leadership, though they are better hidden behind a (temporarily) streamlined façade. This became all too apparent in the examination of the Nazi regime after its downfall. Efficiency may suffer from overconcentration of power, overorganization, flight from responsibility due to fear of reprisals in case something goes wrong, absence of criticism and, consequently, the possibility that vital information never reaches the top level. And finally—as was clearly revealed in the process of "de-Stalinization" in the Soviet Union—if unlimited power makes possible impressive feats, like Soviet industrialization under Stalin or German blitz-rearmament under Hitler, it also opens the way to possible blunders of equal dimensions, such as Hitler's later foreign policy or strategy decisions, or Stalin's wholesale purges and his policies toward the satellite nations.

If democracies are less likely to commit either feats or blunders on such a gigantic scale, it is nevertheless significant that one-man rather than group leadership has characterized most of them in recent times. This is the case not only in democracies with a presidential system, as in the United States, but also in many of those with a cabinet system (which, of course, implies collective leadership), as in Britain. And it is true not only for older countries, but also for new or revamped systems like those of India, Indonesia, Ghana, and West Germany. In fact, it is chiefly in the backwaters of world politics, or in countries like permanently neutralized Switzerland which are artificially shielded from international pressures, that genuine group leadership survives. France used to be the exception which merely proved the rule, for the very fact that its premiers were rarely able to provide forceful leadership under the Fourth Republic was a prime factor in weakening that country and preparing the way for the strong executive of De Gaulle's Fifth Republic.

PROBLEMS OF SELECTION, RESPONSIBILITY, AND SUCCESSION OF THE CHIEF EXECUTIVE

If it is one-man rather than group leadership which characterizes government in our century, this perhaps attests to the importance of speedy and decisive policy-making, especially in foreign and security affairs. This situation throws into high relief, however, the vital import of the selection and responsibility of the supreme holder of power, the process of succession, the selection and responsibility of his chief lieutenants, and the access which they and others have to the leader, whether democratic or dictatorial.

Selection and Responsibility

Turning first to the problem of the selection of a responsible leader, we find that it is democracies rather than dictatorships which are faced with difficult problems. Dictators are self-selective and, in a constitutional sense, irresponsible. Fascist doctrine states this frankly and even boasts of it; the leader is not answerable to "the whims of the masses" but only to "history." Communist theory, it is true, proclaims the responsibility of the leader to the masses whom, even in Leninist doctrine, he is not supposed to leave too far behind. But who decides? Who holds "the vanguard" to its proper task in the absence of institutionalized criticism and control? The revelations about Stalin revealed a leadership which cared little what the masses, even the "class-conscious" proletarians, thought or desired. And if Stalin's rule was attacked by his successors as a monstrous deviation, there was supreme irony in the fact that his main critic, and eventual one-man successor was ousted in turn for having committed grave blunders and, moreover, for having engaged in a "personality cult" along Stalinist lines.

In democracies, on the other hand, the decisive constitutional rules and procedures aim at providing responsible leadership. Whether selection is through direct popular election, as in presidential systems, or indirect, as in parliamentary systems where the vote is cast for a parliamentary party whose leader then becomes head of the government, it is the essence of democracy that the leader thus receive a mandate to which he can be held because it is limited in time. Periodic elections, therefore, are still the indispensable foundation of democratic responsibility.

In a multiparty system like the French under the Fourth Republic, the mandate is less clear than in the British type of two-party system, for the voter does not even know which one among the leading politicians of the various parties will eventually emerge as premier. This problem was less serious than it might appear, however, because the French Cabinet acted as a group, and thus under group policies rather than under one-man leadership, while the French Parliament exercised close control over executive leadership. Whatever disadvantages this had in other respects, it was certainly an effective device for holding the Premier and his colleagues responsible to the popular will, which supposedly resided in the Assembly. This latter check is always a strong factor in the British system, for although the Prime Minister is in many respects in control of Parliament, that body retains, as we have emphasized, the important function of criticism.

On the surface, there is less enforceable responsibility in the presidential system. The American President is free from direct legislative control (though he must work closely with Congress to have his program accepted), and also from the restraints which the collegiate (or cabinet) system provides even in Britain. In this situation, the time limit of his term remains the only vital formal check. Certain informal or less institutionalized ways of rendering account to the public have developed, however, such as the Presidential press conference or the "fireside chat." These attest to the significant role which the press and other channels of mass communications play in modern democracy. Indeed, what would even parliament be in our times without newspapers, radio, and TV reporting to a mass audience on its debates and criticism?

Yet however effective the devices for checks, limitations, and enforcement of responsibility may be in democracies, the job, and therewith necessarily the power, of leadership remain uncomfortably great. This is the more so because of the necessity of granting an even less limited and less clearly defined power to government and, in particular, to the chief executive in time of crisis when only such concentrated power seems able to cope with the emergency. Especially in our times of cataclysmic threats and fears, the temptation to resort to speedy and decisive action is great, and there are few nations, even among the democracies, where emergency powers, martial-law powers, or whatever they may be called, are not tacitly or explicitly provided for. A political theorist, Carl Schmitt, has gone so far as to declare that internal sovereignty belongs to whoever can exercise emergency powers. It is perhaps significant that he is German, for it has been in countries with weak democratic traditions that constitutions have most easily been abrogated or undermined through the use or abuse of emergency powers. But no matter how strong its democratic tradition, no country can afford to disregard the dangers inherent in this problem.

Succession

If democracies have more problems than dictatorships in selecting leaders, the reverse is true when it comes to the matter of succession to leadership positions. In all systems where law determines what happens in government in fact, and not merely in form, succession will proceed in prescribed ways. In a monarchy, succession laws designate the heir to a throne; in a working democracy, the constitution or ordinary statutory law performs the same function in regard to presidents, prime ministers, or other leaders. Ordinarily, in such situations the transition from one leader to another thus proceeds without difficulty. In most democracies, of course, such a change happens in the normal course of regular constitutional procedures as a result of periodic elections.

In dictatorships, on the other hand, succession poses a problem to the very existence of the regime concerned. Since such rule is commonly based upon the "infallible," "unique," and, therefore, "irreplaceable person" of the one and only leader, it is put to its greatest test with his demise. Actually, neither the Nazi nor Fascist dictatorships lived to pass this test, since the death or overthrow of the leader was caused by the forcible action of external enemies. In case of an internal revolt, as in Venezuela or Argentina, it means either the end of the dictatorship as such or the establishment of a new one on the basis of the successor's "charisma."

But after a dictator's death, as with Lenin in 1924 and Stalin in 1953, the transmission of his halo to a successor is a difficult task. It might be facilitated by a formal sanction already given to the future successor by the dictator during his own lifetime, but this creates a "crown-prince problem," and totalitarian leaders, from Mussolini and Hitler to Stalin, have been loath to take such action. Franco, on the other hand, has long prepared to meet this problem, not by selecting a successor to the dictatorship, but rather through preparing for a return of the monarchy. In Stalin's case (assuming his death was natural) transmission of power was relatively smooth on the surface, but, as we now know, it involved a series of struggles for power before Khrushchev emerged as the undisputed leader. In contrast, the ousting of Khrushchev and the succession to his powers was both quick and apparently without grave repercussions.

If, as is obvious, the sharpest contrasts over succession are between dictatorial and democratic regimes, it should also be noted that different types of constitutional systems produce their own characteristic ways of providing for the succession of their leaders. The Presidential elections in the American system provide not only the chief executive but, simultaneously, the leader of the party whose nominee is installed in the White

House; though most American Presidents have had experience as members of Congress, or perhaps more often, as state governors, neither is mandatory, as General Eisenhower's election in 1952 proved. In the British type of parliamentary government, in contrast, the Prime Minister is the leader of the party which wins a majority of the seats; inevitably, he has had parliamentary experience and, almost inevitably (Winston Churchill proved an exception), he has headed the party organization for a considerable time.

A party leader may be chosen by the parliamentary members of the party, as is the practice in Great Britain, Australia, New Zealand, and South Africa, or by a party convention, as is done in Canada or in most Continental European countries. In either case, it takes a palace revolution to unseat him once he is selected. It is true that the Canadian Progressive Conservative Party picked three leaders in the space of sixteen years, hoping each time to find one who could lead them to victory, as did John Diefenbaker in 1957, to end temporarily a twenty-two year period of office by the Liberals. The Australian Labour Party also twice renounced its leaders, once during World War I and once in the Depression, when they were already serving as Prime Ministers, but in both instances it was the party, not the leaders, who lost office. But these are exceptions, as was Churchill's elevation to office in 1941, and normally the leaders of conservative, liberal, and labor parliamentary parties have long tenures of office. Thus, they bring to the highest executive office, when they achieve it, a breadth of experience in parliamentary and party affairs which few American Presidents can rival.

Moreover, the British-type parliamentary system grooms aspirants for office through the grueling responsibilities of leading the opposition. There is thus ample guarantee for training and experience of leadership. In Continental countries, on the other hand, there is frequently a greater turnover of party leaders, especially in multiparty systems, and thus less likelihood of leaders acquiring both forcefulness and experience. We even find an occasional separation of party leadership from the leadership in government of the governing party; thus, when Adenauer resigned his Chancellorship in favor of Ludwig Erhard, he was allowed to retain the chairmanship of Germany's Christian Democratic Party. Quite obviously, such a duality obfuscates the question of who directs policies and who is accountable to whom, and thus may result in dangerous conflict at the top level of political leadership.

In the United States, on the other hand, the absence of organized and centrally led parliamentary opposition has meant that a defeated Presidential candidate generally has only a nominal and politically meaningless leadership function, especially in cases where defeat has discredited him as a leader. The minority party then usually turns to someone new for leadership in the next election. Thus, somewhat paradoxically, the system which, potentially, vests the greatest authority of any democratic country in a single figure does least to provide training and experience for the tremendous responsibilities of the Presidency.

Among the new countries, the problem of succession is made more difficult by the relatively small number of people capable of assuming such responsibilities. Any country may have a charismatic leader—and in any system the demands on and the response to leadership will depend greatly on whether the leader is charismatic or not—but the importance of personality is particularly great where there is little sense of national unity and the party structure is fairly rudimentary. Instead of being organizational, as in more developed democracies, leadership in the new states tends to be personal and even self-selected (but rather through ability to hold conflicting groups together than through a struggle for power). The steady disintegration of the Moslem League and its inability to provide coherent direction in Pakistan after the death of one leader and the assas- sination of another illustrates the great dependence of party organization on leadership in newly developing states. Not only is there a disturbing reliance on one or a few leaders to hold together political organization and to direct development, but, almost as a corollary which reflects the uncertainty about the succession, a degree of haste in achieving results which may threaten constitutional procedures. In both respects, the early years of independence are crucial, and if these are successfully negotiated, the country may acquire a more stable social unity and more settled patterns of action able to survive the strains and divisions which, as we have seen, have tilted the balance toward at least temporary army rule in several Asian countries and the Sudan.

The Selection and Responsibility of Lieutenants

The differences between the ways democratic and totalitarian states select political lieutenants are even more striking than are those in the selection of chief executives. Where political lieutenants obviously share power, as do the members of the cabinet in parliamentary systems, they are formally appointed by the chief executive or (as is the case in Australia when the Labour Party is in office) selected by the caucus, i.e., the parliamentary members of the party. Under the doctrine of collective responsibility, everyone in the cabinet not only considers but also must publicly support government policy. If a minister wishes to oppose a policy outside the walls of the cabinet chamber, he must resign to do so. So long as he is in office, however, he both runs his department and assumes full responsibility for its policies before parliament and the public. The American Cabinet is also composed of political heads of departments, but it is a pale reflection of the British or Australian Cabinet as far as sharing power is concerned, for the extent of its members' responsibilities and policy-making depends on the will of the particular President. Under President Eisenhower, for example, John Foster Dulles had virtually unlimited discretion in the field of foreign affairs, while his successor, Christian Herter, had relatively little. Cabinets in multiparty systems like that of the Fourth French Republic reflect impermanent coalitions, but for this very reason a minister may possess more independent authority than a British cabinet minister, since in the multiparty system he is usually an individual of competence, as well as the representative of a party whose support is essential to the life of the coalition. Moreover, in the realm of foreign affairs, for example, the tenure of a minister in the Fourth French Republic was often far longer than that of the Premier. Under the Fifth Republic, the concentration of power in the executive, the fact that a minister may not hold a seat in the legislature, and the tendency to use civil servants as ministers, have produced a situation in which the French Cabinet is more like the American than the British, while the chambers are far less vigorous than in either of these two countries. The same holds for West Germany, where the Chancellor, once he has been appointed by majority vote of parliament, has the power (vigorously used by Adenauer throughout his tenure) to appoint, shift, and dismiss ministers without concern for parliament or even, in cases where the minister was of his own party, for his party's approval.

In totalitarian states, lieutenants to the dictator occupy a far more equivocal position than do cabinet members in democratic states. Their selection is a reflection of the internal power struggle at a given moment. Even when the dictator seems to occupy an unquestioned position of authority, shifts go on—as was seen throughout Stalin's regime—which exalt one person temporarily and then cause his disappearance or demotion. China is notable for the constancy with which its top figures, in particular Mao Tse-tung and Chou En-lai, have worked together, but most Communist states have felt the impact of the permanent purge or of the struggle for ultimate succession all the way to the highest levels.

INFORMAL CHANNELS OF ACCESS TO THE LEADER

In a period when government seems to consist largely of impersonal regulations applied to vast numbers of similar cases and situations, it may appear strange to put great weight on questions like: Who has the ear of a president? Who is most influential in the cabinet surrounding a prime minister? We expect camarillas to play their role in uncontrolled dictatorships, but in other systems stories of personal influence and intrigue in high places, of "gray eminences" and ruling mistresses seem to belong to a past of dynastic and similar personal rule. Yet personal friendship, kitchen cabinets, and similar influences have never ceased to play a role in democratic as well as in dictatorial systems. The problem has indeed gained new significance with the heightened tasks of political leadership and the increased urgency and secrecy surrounding it in the age of nuclear insecurity.

The area of governmental secrecy has grown increasingly for security and related reasons. The top level of policy-making has, of course, always been conducted in secrecy, even in the most advanced democracies, as witness the meetings and discussions of the British Cabinet, or those of the American Cabinet and National Security Council. This is inevitable if there is to be free and frank discussion before policy decisions are taken.

But while participation in such bodies is highly important, we discover from time to time that their members are not necessarily those whose words will be most influential on ultimate decisions. Department or agency heads in the United States or even Cabinet Ministers in Great Britain may be less influential, in practice, than unofficial aides, friends, or lieutenants, especially where, despite the enormous growth of his functions and powers, the leader is not provided with an appropriate official staff of his own. More important than top-ranking official advisers may be secretaries, appointment officers, or special or personal assistants, like a Sherman Adams, under Eisenhower, in Washington, or a Hans Globke, under Adenauer, in Bonn. The mere fact of a chief executive's limited time points up the problem. Policy decisions may depend on the appointment calendar, that is, on who gains access to the holder of power and who does not, or on what the leader hears and reads and what he does not. Connected with this is the problem that looms so large these days—how best to coordinate "intelligence." The leader can absorb only so much; what is selected, and in what form it is presented, may determine his action or inaction, with far-reaching results. Instead of emphasizing the vast powers of the leader in a modern industrial state, some observers stress that the chief executive, perhaps particularly in the United States, is the prisoner of his staff. All the more reason, therefore, to give executives the maximum aid of highly responsible assistants, and to encourage the kind of inquisitiveness into the wide range of governmental affairs that keeps ultimate decision-making in the hands of those to whom the public has entrusted that responsibility.

The Role and Selection of the Bureaucracy

The higher bureaucracy is as important in providing advice, aid, and also policy proposals as is the second line of executive leadership, the ministers. No man can hope to keep abreast of the multitudinous factors of modern administration. One of the most important talents a leader must have is the ability to delegate powers, although, if he is to fulfill his mandate from the people, he must also retain ultimate responsibility. The chief executive is also and necessarily the head of the administration. But in democratic states, the administration carries not only the responsibility of executing the laws, but also of seeing that they fulfill the purposes for which they were designed. Thus the administration, and particularly the higher bureaucracy, must be constantly alert both to the purposes of the political leaders of the country and to the needs as well as desires of the public.

This view of the role of the bureaucracy, which is now generally accepted in democratic states, was disputed in earlier times. The Prussian and subsequently Imperial German view was that serving the purposes of the state rather than providing services for the people was the primary duty of public administration. This concept had the advantage of establishing clear-cut and single-minded responsibility to the monarch, and it was saved from promoting arbitrariness by the insistence on the *Rechtsstaat*, the rule of law. It has been one of the reasons why, to this day, the ministerial bureaucracy in West Germany predominates in many political processes, especially vis-à-vis the legislature. But this view fitted ill with the notions of popular sovereignty characteristic of the French Revolution. Under their impact, law came to be regarded not merely as the will of the state, enunciated by its supreme figure, but as a collection of rules devised for the better organization of the affairs of the community. In this perspective, public power became transmuted into public service.

In France, syndicalism went a step further, maintaining that public employees were no different from private employees and should have the right, therefore, to organize in trade unions, engage in political activity, and publicly express their opinions even if these were contrary to those of the political leaders. But activities along these lines were among the factors that weakened Italy and Spain in their pre-Fascist period and facilitated the accession of authoritarianism; they were not without effect in undermining the postwar Fourth French Republic. What may be termed the public-service state, at least in countries following the Anglo-Saxon tradition, now, therefore, endorses these views: that the interests of the public are superior to those of any group of public servants; that employment by the state differs from private employment in the techniques and tactics which it is legitimate to use in attempting to change conditions of service (in particular, strikes are not an acceptable means of pressure); and that, while government employees should have the right to exercise the franchise in their private capacities, there is a basic incompatibility between government employment and open political activity, at least at the level of government (i.e., local or national) in which service is being rendered.

These distinctions, it must be admitted, make much less sense in jobs comparable to those in private service than in jobs that are unique to public service. In cases where some sectors of the economy are nationalized, there would seem little reason for treating their employees differently than would be the case if the services were privately supported—except for the fact that nationalization either creates or grows out of monopolies and often in spheres which provide essential public services, like transportation. Thus a strike in a nationalized industry or service, like coal mining or air transportation, has far more impact on the country as a whole than would a strike against an individual enterprise. Nonetheless, as government spreads into new areas of activity, there is increasing reason to separate what might be called genuine public-law and basically private-law employment and to treat them differently. Few people can doubt, however, that special provisions and traditions are essential for the type of government employment for which there is no parallel in business.

But if there is agreement on this fact, there are wide differences in the ways democratic states have handled problems of selection, training, and promotion, particularly for that all-important group, the higher bureaucracy, which is involved in policy-making almost as much as in administration. The British deliberately recruit personnel for particular types of responsibilities and select most candidates for the top grades with the help of written and oral tests which seek to evaluate the intellectual capacities and character of outstanding university graduates. Unlike most other countries—except those of the older and some of the newer members of the Commonwealth overseas—the British choose the highest departmental officials from the permanent service, thus making it a career service of great distinction, although they run the possible danger of substituting ability for genuine sympathy with the programs being introduced. Americans, on the other hand, have never wholly discarded their belief that practical experience in business or commerce may be more useful in government service than academically tested ability and long experience. Although it is more common these days to find top officials retaining their posts (particularly posts requiring technical skills) despite a change in administration, there is far more infiltration from outside into all ranks of government service than is the case in Great Britain or in European countries. This can be particularly valuable when a "new deal" is instituted and knowledge is combined with enthusiasm in those most concerned with introducing new measures, but it also limits the attractiveness of public service as a career. Moreover, the number of short-term "political" appointments, particularly under Republican administrations, makes decisiveness and continuity of policy difficult. Furthermore, in systems like the American, there are the dangers ever inherent in "patronage"—that is, the practice antedating the establishment of a genuine "merit" system of civil service, in which public office is used to reward unqualified persons to whom party leaders are obligated politically or possibly financially (e.g., for contributions to campaign funds), or of appointing those who, in turn, will be beholden to the person making the appointment or to the party for their jobs. In such circumstances, by no means uncommon in other countries also, the danger of corruption—whether in the moral or even the criminal sense—is always present. Even without this danger, however, there is the not inconsiderable one—particularly in the field of foreign service—of jeopardizing the national interest through inexperienced or incompetent representatives.

The French use academic tests based on specialized training for their higher administrators, who often perform tasks that in British administration are delegated to the executive or "sergeant-major" level, as well as more characteristically directive ones, simply because the French service is less strong at the second-highest level. In addition, however, a minister brings with him his own "cabinet" of administrators who work with the regular departmental officials to see that the minister's policies are carried out in accordance with his wishes.

Other, more subtle differences may result from the class structure and the prestige of the higher civil service. If, as was long true in Great Britain, ministers and the higher bureaucracy are drawn from a certain group of families, schools, and universities they tend to have similar implicit assumptions about how policy should be executed; however, the British Labour Party, upon assuming office, found it could also work well with the higher civil servants. But such a degree of national consensus on essentials did not exist in Weimar Germany, where the permanent service hampered, and even impeded, the implementation of democratically inclined or socially advanced policies, and thus contributed to that regime's weakness and ultimate collapse in 1933. The less class-conscious and more equalitarian American educational system leads to a more differentiated, if less intellectually inclined, higher public service than exists in either Great Britain, France, or Germany; though this has the advantage of representativeness, it does not balance the limitations of less marked ability.

The prestige a bureaucracy enjoys also has a bearing on the type of person it is able to attract. In Germany, the public official has greater status than in any other European country, or possibly any place else, both a reflection of a belief in the expert and an identification of bureaucracy with the state. In Sweden, Denmark, and Holland, he is trusted, but he is not regarded with anything like the same deference. The Swiss, French, Italians, and Spanish are openly critical of their public servants, though the last two with more reason than the first. Americans, with their traditional idealization of the businessman, are only gradually acquiring the degree of respect for public service which the British have long held, and they are also learning that such respect and the standards of the service tend to reinforce each other.

If such factors are so influential, can it be said that the higher civil service is ever neutral in its attitudes toward public questions? Perhaps not; but should it be? The kind of issues dealt with by the top level of bureaucrats for the most part are not those which can be handled by reference to rules. They are policy-raising issues for which no legislature and no executive can provide all the directives. Higher civil servants are confronted constantly by the need to use their own discretion in determining how best to carry out a policy so that its results will be in the public interest. This necessitates a sensitivity to tensions within the community and to genuine needs, as opposed to spurious claims, which taxes every faculty. The best members of the higher bureaucracy are likely to be those who are not hidebound either by ideology or by special class interests, public servants who can retain an open mind and a sympathetic understanding of public needs and purposes. If, as is true in democratic states, the public servant is immediately responsible to the elected executive, the ultimate responsibility of both is to the people.

Bureaucracy in the New States

Nowhere are administrative skill, experience, and public responsibility more needed than in the new states. Their very poverty of material resources and accumulated capital thrusts upon them a multitude of tasks in their efforts to become "modern." Almost all these tasks must be directed or supervised by the public service. Yet it is generally in this field that their needs are greatest. The five hundred top Indian administrators who, up to the time India attained independence, shared the subcontinent's major governmental responsibilities with an equal number from Great Britain itself, constituted perhaps the most valuable heritage of British rule in India. That Pakistan could claim only about seventy of those trained for high posts under British rule caused major difficulties in Pakistan's task of administrative construction and contributed to the laxities that paved the way for army rule. The fact that India had more than four hundred trained administrators on whom it could depend was of vast help in its early years of independence and its ambitious development projects. Compared to both these countries, the African countries that have achieved independence have been handicapped indeed. The Africanization of administrative services did not start on any scale until after World War II, and, in all too many cases, has been accelerated at the expense of training and quality.

Many of the new African states, including Ghana, which had some of the best African administrative talent at independence in 1957, have found it necessary to increase the number of white employees in their public service, reflecting the fact that African advance could not keep up with the expansion of responsibilities brought on by large-scale development. When the Belgians in the Congo so hastily withdrew from their responsibilities to grant independence in June, 1960, the most serious lack was that of African administrators. In the British and French territories in Africa, arrangements have commonly been made with former colonial officials to remain in office until Africans were trained to take their places; in the Congo, the lack of confidence on both sides led to premature withdrawal. When the United Nations had to step in to re-establish order, its personnel also restarted essential services, a fact that points to the importance of establishing a substantial international civil service to aid the developing countries.

The new states face special handicaps in building their administrative services. Their educational structures taper quickly to the point of the pyramid; in other words, even where primary education is widespread, as is increasingly the case, secondary and higher educational facilities remain minimal. Those who succeed in completing secondary schools frequently go on through university, thereby increasing the numbers available for professional administrative posts, but this leaves almost no one to fill the highly important secondary rung of executive and even secretarial posts. A further problem arises from the need to replace traditional family-oriented loyalties by loyalty to the state. Traditional norms in many non-Western societies demand what we condemn as nepotism, that is, providing jobs for family members; there is also a less sharp differentiation between public money and private money. There is the further problem, particularly in Africa, that if one member of a family has a well-paid post, his relatives assume that he will support them.

The colonial bureaucracies have set a high standard of probity and devotion to duty, which countries like Nigeria expect their own administrators to follow. The transfer of authority to local hands, however, requires a major adjustment in the thinking of the most upright bureaucracy, for independence not only means a local center of power; it also means that bureaucracy is responsible to that center of power instead of having virtually unlimited discretion in its own hands. Thus, even where administrative skills exist, the new states have their own particular problems in developing the kind of relationship between the elected executive and the public administration that befits a democratically organized state. In the light of all these difficulties and of the great pressures for development, the achievements of the new states rather than their shortcomings should be highlighted.

Bureaucracy in Totalitarian States

Totalitarian states face an inherent dilemma in regard to their administrative services. They depend on them far more than would any democratic state, particularly one in whose economy private enterprise assumes a major role. Their very dependence on administrators to manage the economy as well as all other services, however, runs contrary to the concentration of power in the hands of the party. Moreover, efficient administration dictates its own rules of organization, i.e., fixed jurisdictions, hierarchical chain of command, reliance on written orders, dependence on specialists, and stable routines. Yet this regularity contrasts sharply with the pressures of what we have called the permanent purge. In other words, the two major means whereby totalitarian states, and in particular the Soviet Union, control all aspects of life—the bureaucracy and the party—require opposing conditions for their maximum effectiveness: the former, stability; the latter, constant ferment.

These counterpulls have evidenced themselves throughout the history of the Soviet Union. Marxist dogma, of course, condemned bureaucracy as an instrument of bourgeois oppression. Lenin originally thought the workers themselves would be able to administer the state and industry. Since the importance of administrative skills and responsibility quickly became apparent in the Soviet state, however, party members were assigned to watch over managerial operations. Under the Five-Year Plans, the channels for the great industrial expansion of the Soviet Union, professional administrators began to achieve a privileged status, and they became important party members. Even then, however, they were exposed periodically to impossible demands and to the fear of punishment for failure to meet them. In order to fulfill their quotas, ministries would try to corral supplies, transport, and labor. Khrushchev himself was our authority on some of the resulting absurdities which led to duplication of effort in some instances and lack of use of resources in others (such as one ministry moving goods in its own ships in one direction only and allowing them to return empty when another ministry was doing exactly the same in the opposite direction). Khrushchev's own administrative reorganization in 1957 sought to avoid such waste by breaking up the top-heavy ministries centralized in Moscow under the Stalinist regime. Still more important from his point of view, however, the reorganization undercut the power of the managerial class, broke up the bureaucratic concentration in the capital, and brought industry under the control of well-entrenched regional party agents. As with so many other policies which Khrushchev promoted, this one was designed to enhance the power of the party by simplifying its task of maintaining supervision over the economic bureaucracy, that is, that part of the administration which directs industry. Yet inevitably, the new administrative patterns which developed are also solidifying. Thus the contest continues, with ultimate political power firmly vested in party hands, but the rationale of a heavily bureaucratized state exerting its own constant pressures toward stability.

The Role of Pressure Groups

Modern "pluralistic" society, which is dynamic and consists of large numbers of economic, occupational, religious, possibly ethnic, and other groups, inevitably confronts the problem of the relation between these "interests" and those of government and politics. In an open society, interest groups will be permitted freely to organize themselves; they will, therefore, not only engage in an interplay of forces vis-à-vis each other (such as employers and employees in worker-manager relations) but will also tend to bring their influence to bear on the machinery and the processes of government, which influences them so much through laws, rulings, licenses, taxation, and innumerable other legislative and administrative acts. As seen from the point of view of the latter, "interests" thus turn into "pressure groups," and their activities into pressures upon government. Indeed, "group theory" in political science has tended to interpret almost everything which goes on in government and politics as the outgrowth of the interplay between interest groups, on the one hand, and government, on the other. While the effect of this interplay may be exaggerated, it is advisable not to commit the opposite mistake and, as political scientists did for a long time, either underestimate or neglect the role of pressure groups.

In speaking earlier of the way in which influence is brought to bear on key men, particularly the top figures in the executive and the administration, we mentioned the influence of aides and advisers, and the importance of their recruitment, their access to the leader, etc. But the general problem of influence in government is more complex, and has more dimensions than we have so far indicated. Every administration, whether democratic or dictatorial, has its own internal rivalries, strains, and divisions of opinion. Some of these strains derive from self-seeking, some from genuine differences of view among leaders or the parties they represent, some from overspecialization, and others from lack of knowledge and experience. Finally, there are some strains—and these may be particularly important—which are the result of outside influences and pressures.

Many people feel that pressure groups are necessarily harmful, because they seek to exalt the interests of small, though possibly wealthy or highly organized segments of the population, disregarding the interests of all or of a substantial segment of the people. But this view is not necessarily correct. Much depends, in this respect, on whether *all* interest groups, and not only the more powerful and better organized ones, get a hearing, and, second, on whether these groups, in their own internal organizations, function in such a way that their entire membership rather than entrenched oligarchies determine their policies. In other words, it is a question of how much democracy, in the sense of responsibleness, there is in the internal structure of these groups, as well as in their relation to government and society at large.

It must thus be one of the objectives of political democracies to bring into the open the pressures of influence groups, so that their source and impact can be evaluated by the general public. Public responsibility requires sufficient openness about how political and administrative decisions are reached, so that undue influence can be corrected. It is one of the main shortcomings of nondemocratic systems that the pressures, which do exist in fact even under the most centralized dictatorial controls, are kept secret, so that the people have no way of knowing who is in charge and responsible for what.

Where they work in the open, however, pressure groups fulfill a necessary and potentially wholesome function. They may form a link between the people and the government of which administrators or legislators can make use to secure information on facts and attitudes. For example, any democratic government would expect to consult farmers' organizations before instituting new farm programs and also in evaluating existing ones. As a matter of fact, lobbying can claim to follow two essentially democratic procedures: the right to participate in the formulation of policy and the right to redress of grievances. So long as pressure groups are not permitted to usurp the political function, their specialized knowledge of attitudes and facts can provide that connection between the ruled and the rulers without which the latter cannot be responsible to its public. Thus the problem created by pressure groups is not that they are consulted, but that they sometimes force their will upon legislators or administrators. Under these latter circumstances they may not only lower standards of public morality but also distort to their own advantage policy which is or should be designed for the public interest, or at least should constitute a fair compromise of conflicting interests of opposing groups.

In actual fact, this danger of distortion can become great in countries with highly organized interest groups, some of which have developed the techniques of influence into a fine art. Where, in addition to this situation, the public has become used to such practices, expects them as a matter of course, and accepts their effects without much questioning, politics threatens to degenerate into a mere "Who gets what, when, and how." More, perhaps, than in other countries, pressure groups have, in fact, become something of a fifth estate in the American system of government, and it is not without reason that the most detailed studies of pressure groups and pressure politics have been of those which operate on the American scene—which in itself provides some safeguards through the resulting publicity of pressure-group activities.

The American party system, with its lack of centralization (except at election time), of discipline, and of firm leadership, lends itself to the pressures of special-interest groups. So, too, does the separation of powers, which opens the way to exploiting not only rivalries, but what is often a disturbing lack of communication and integration between, and even within, the different branches. Moreover, the public passively acquiesces, for the most part, in the open tug of war between rival interest groups and, in what may be still more costly, alliances between them through which potentially conflicting claims are resolved in a manner detrimental to the public interest. Management and labor, for example, might agree on large wage increases, but such an agreement could run counter to the interests of consumers in preventing higher prices and consequent inflationary pressures; lobbies may combine in order to raise tariffs, with some of the same results.

Because economic concentration has gone so far in the United States, there is constant suspicion among liberals that political power is subject to economic power, whether exercised through open lobbying or through the influence of businessmen who hold high office in the administration for a period of time, or through dubious practices. According to the Communists, of course, government in a capitalist economy inevitably becomes an instrument in the hands of dominant economic interests and the political leaders become the "running dogs" of the bourgeoisie. While this view grossly exaggerates the impact of economic power, there can be little question that corporate wealth does influence the power of government. In Great Britain, France, and Germany, as well as in the United States, administrators find it more convenient to consult with big business and its representatives than with the multitude of small ones. The organizations of the former are more streamlined, their information more clearly defined, their actions more predictable. Beyond this, the resources of big corporations make it possible to exert pressure on the many rungs of the American administrative and legislative processes. So, too, do the sources of the big labor unions, some of which have as marked a concentration of authority as do corporations.

It is significant to note that interest groups may also exert pressure for change through the judicial system, the most striking example being the successful effort of the National Association for the Advancement of Colored People to secure the judgment by the Supreme Court that the segregation of schools is unconstitutional. On the whole, however, pressure groups concentrate on the administrative bureaus or ministries and on committee chairmen and party leaders. Many of the proposals for new public policy come from such pressure groups, it must be noted, but on balance it seems as if pressure politics had less effect through causing innovations than through preventing change. The long campaign against national health insurance in the United States has been a classic example of the latter process.

If the party and governmental systems in the United States facilitate the impact of private pressures on policy-making, the strength of the national consensus limits to some extent their divisive effect. But in France under the Fourth Republic, the situation was more serious. The growing lack of discipline in the political parties, other than the Communists, opened the way for an ever-increasing influence by pressure groups, particularly those of the business lobby, until at times it surpassed that of the parties themselves, while the lack of public agreement on political and social values provided a milieu in which conflict became exaggerated rather than resolved. In Great Britain, in contrast, a highly structured bureaucracy and highly disciplined political parties keep the decision-making process firmly in control, and pressure groups become a major means of keeping constantly in touch with a wide variety of attitudes toward public policy.

It appears, therefore, that the strength or weakness of the political decision-making process is of great significance for the role pressure groups can play in the respective political systems. In addition, the type of the political system has a good deal to do with the way in which pressures operate. In that variety of the parliamentary system under which basic decisions are made at the top level of the executive rather than in parliament, as in Great Britain or West Germany—i.e., where most bills originate with the respective executive departments and their ministerial bureaucracy—the pressure group lobbyists are more likely to besiege the executive than the members of parliament. Where, as traditionally in France before the Fifth Republic and now in Italy, the legislature predominates at least in the lawmaking process, the deputies bear the brunt. Under a system of separate powers, as in the United States, pressures are likely to affect both branches equally. Likewise, the way in which parties represent or reflect particular interests has a bearing on the chances and methods of pressures. Where, as in the United States, both major parties appeal to all the major strata of society, pressures operate on and within both. What becomes particularly important then are whom an individual Congressman or member of a state legislature represents, how susceptible he is to influence, and so forth. Where, as in Britain, the two major parties represent (among others) two distinct classes and their interests, these two parties, in a way, function themselves as interest groups. This fact becomes clear when one counts the number of trade unionists among Labour MP's or of businessmen among Conservative MP's. In a system like the German, where, even more than in Great Britain, the individual members of interest groups (such as industrialists or farmers) tend to leave the representation of their interests to professionals, one is not surprised to find a substantial number of officials of professional and occupational organizations serving as elected deputies in parliament; the same is true in Japan. Thus the lobby, so to speak, invades and infiltrates the representative machinery itself.

The "take-over" phenomenon, however, is not limited to the legislature. To the extent that executive departments are set up to deal with specific areas of the economy (e.g., labor, commerce, and agriculture), they may come to be considered, and themselves act as if they were, servants of the corresponding interests (e.g., outposts of the trade unions, the business community, or the big farmers' organizations). To some extent this is legitimate, but if the top incumbents forget that in addition to safeguarding the interests of their clientele they must also protect those of the public as a whole and implement over-all policies of the government as such, the danger arises that the government may become merely the arena of a fight in which opposing forces and interests pull hither and thither and the common weal is submerged.

Yet the top level of government usually has a better chance of combating undue pressure than the local level. A local community anxious to keep an industrial enterprise and the employment it provides may be pressured into not taxing it enough to help to provide for decent schooling or urban renewal, or into closing its eyes when that factory pollutes its river. A ministry is not under such direct pressure. This is another reason why, if the great community tasks of our age are to be taken care of efficiently, they must be at least supervised by the central government.

In this connection, too, the type and attitude of leadership will be decisive. Especially in a country like the United States, where the parties are the chief representatives of competing interests, the national mandate of the Presidency is of utmost importance. If there is no integration of the plurality of groups and interests at this point, there will be none at all. Still, the American system, where interests, although working in and through parties, are not organized *as* parties, is at an advantage compared with systems where coalition governments made up from interest parties have difficulty in rising above a mere dividing up of the commonwealth to their own advantage.

Much also depends, in this connection, upon the social origin of the political elite. In countries where, as until recently in Britain and still largely in Germany, political leadership is restricted to an educated class drawn from a relatively small upper stratum, leadership easily identifies national interest with that of narrower groups and classes. But this is not necessarily the case. Not infrequently, a feeling of *noblesse oblige* leads persons of aristocratic or similar upper-class backgrounds to act in a more broadminded, liberal, and even democratic way than those from a lower stratum would do. This has been true in America, too. More democracy in the selection of the political elite has not always resulted in less personal, social, or similar bias. At the same time, while European countries may display class restrictions in selection, the "classless" society of the United States still manifests actual, though not legal, restrictions based on racial origin or religious affiliation.

A free world engaged in competition with a system where a jungle type of struggle for political survival tends to bring the most ruthless to the fore can hardly afford to place restrictions on the selection of the ablest among its citizens. It is, therefore, confronted with a twofold educational problem: first, how to educate the citizenry so that, free from bias and un-affected by the hullabaloo of the hucksters, it will make intelligent choices; and second, in what amounts to a modern version of the age-old problem of the "education of the prince," how to develop in its potential leaders that combination of knowledge and ability out of which they will act both with authority and with responsibility, the hallmarks of democratic leadership.

VII

BELIEF SYSTEMS AND POLITICS

THE ROLE OF IDEOLOGY

At the beginning of this book, we pointed out that the deepest challenge of totalitarianism lies in its claim that it alone can fill the spiritual void left by the decline of established religion in the modern age. Beyond their material wants, men need a belief in the meaningfulness of their lives, a faith in some higher cause to which they as individuals as well as the groups to which they belong can be devoted. Many believe that in this period of change and crisis, liberal democracy is failing to answer this need.

Behind these issues lies another problem. It can be summed up in these questions: What ties political communities together? What is it that forms those feelings and attitudes of attachment to the group, that minimum of allegiance without which a political community can neither be established nor endure? In this era of numerous and strongly divisive views, interests, and even centers of allegiance, what gives cohesion to a political community?

We in the West have long ignored this problem, largely because we have been under the influence of individualism, that mainstream of modern social and political thought. Whether it bases itself upon the concept of an original social or political contract or upon the concept of utility, individualism has assumed that political units, like nation-states, are founded upon, or could and should be founded upon, the free and voluntary association of self-determining, rational, enlightened human beings.

But Burke, two centuries ago, pointed out that a country is more than a utilitarian or contractual association; that its cohesion rests less on interests and is less braced by reason than it is founded on custom and tradition; and that even prejudice may serve to preserve "the ancient order into which we are born." To many moderns this may sound like tribalism; but even Rousseau, who differed from Burke in so many respects, called for a "civil religion" so that the "general will" of a free community would be sure to prevail.

To talk of maintaining or even instilling the right prejudices, or of enforcing a civil religion, points up a basic dilemma in the relations between the individual and the community. We have been apt to forget that the attempt to render the individual autonomous and to make him the foundation of free communities and limited government has been relatively rare and recent in history. For during most of the history even of Western Europe, and of most of the world until the present or the recent past, political communities, however they were first established (i.e., by war, by conquest, or occasionally by free compact), have been kept together by an unquestioning, traditionalist allegiance of the ruled to the rulers. Generally, there was no conscious effort to indoctrinate the people, nor even to mold their attitudes and opinions through formal education; this was not necessary. It was the prevailing atmosphere, the transmitted value and belief systems, which provided these standards. And it was in large part the churches which provided whatever institutional and organizational apparatus was required to ensure their hold.

With the era of the Enlightenment came a change in attitude. To many people it seemed desirable to conduct human affairs on the basis of conscious, deliberate, and free acceptance of value standards, whether they eventually turned out to be religious or not. Loyalty freely given, so one believed, provides a stronger and more democratic foundation of nations than does an enforced allegiance—or even a less consciously and more traditionally established allegiance. Thus, such loyalty has become the truly democratic ideal.

Frequently, however, it is only the few who know how to develop their own personal beliefs and how to make these beliefs the basis of living together with others in political communities. This explains why, after traditional authoritarian rulership has lost its grip, it is often a new irrational emotion, nationalism, which ensures the cohesion of existing units or makes for the formation of new ones. When nationalism was simply a moderate and relatively calm feeling of belonging to that group which constitutes the nation, it could still be reconciled with a liberal-democratic individualism. But to the extent that nationalism became the substitute religion of those who needed or were possessed of more extreme and fervent feelings of attachment, it became a focal point for emphatic identification with one group, and antagonism, even hatred, toward all others. Thus nationalism has all too easily been converted into an ideology of exclusivism and, in a variety of forms (racialism, bellicism, imperialism, Social Darwinism, political romanticism), has eventually become the doctrinal foundation of various totalitarian movements, most particularly Italian Fascism and the even more extreme movement of Nazism.

Nationalism is one basis of modern totalitarian ideology. Another basis has been the need for a coherent philosophy of government and politics, a political *Weltanschauung*, which arises once the masses of the people have been called upon to participate in politics. It is well known how this need contributed to the appeal of Nazism; but we should note that even in the nineteenth century it had led rising and unattached proletarian groups in Germany and elsewhere to embrace the new Marxian creed and movement. And as we know full well, the crises, strains, and stresses of our century have contributed far more widely to the appeal of the other major type of totalitarian ideology, Communism—particularly since this philosophy has a rational or quasi-rational appeal through its allegedly scientific explanation of historical evolution and current conditions, which draws to it many who would reject the irrational mysticism and the racial or nationalist fanaticism of fascism.

But the yearning for a belief system and a movement with a cause can also be found in more Western and less extreme climes. It is observable in some degree in most mass parties, whether that of British Labour or the more leftist among French or Italian parties. It reflects the *anomie* (the lack of basic rules or standards of value) of individuals lost in the maze of modern mass society who have become alienated from traditional ways of life without having found safe new ones.

Confronted with the weakening of social ties which *anomie* represents in its most extreme form, democracy runs two opposite dangers. If it sticks to its liberal ideal and leaves the individual free to choose among standards and causes without direction, the plurality of interests and creeds of modern society may lead to such disunity as to endanger the cohesion of the political unit. In the extreme case, it may even lead to the internecine warfare of armed ideologies; or, at the least, result in sheer political opportunism, which is likewise a doubtful basis for national cohesion. The other and opposite danger is that the effort may be made to instill loyalty from above, to indoctrinate the citizen and especially the younger generation with whatever civil religion seems appropriate. This obviously leads to the evils of conformity and to the undermining of the liberalism with which democracy is so intimately bound up.

To avoid the horns of this dilemma requires wise judgment and constant vigilance. The middle way between the two extremes is made easier where nations enjoy the absence of deep class divisions, the maturity of a people used to developing its own standards, and relative security from outside dangers.

Here the impact of international developments is obvious. As long as nation-states still enjoyed a fair measure of security, they needed less emotional attachment on the part of their citizens for their internal cohesion than do present-day, more insecure, units. In the absence of security, it is tempting to ensure an iron unity through uniformity of creed, a pattern perhaps less virulent than, but nevertheless with elements of, totalitarianism.

However, totalitarian regimes run into troubles of their own. There seems to be a law of diminishing returns in regard to indoctrination. Though individuals in a mass society long for safe beliefs, yet they are easily satiated when doctrines are too emphatically instilled or when, in the present conflict of systems and ideologies, one has replaced another in bewildering sequence.

Consider the case of the young Pole who told an American journalist (*The New York Times,* May 11, 1956):

> When I was ten, I ceased to believe in my fatherland. I had God. When I was fifteen, I ceased to believe in God. . . . A friend gave me help. He was a Communist. He restored my faith in mankind. These were my happiest years. . . . Now it has turned out that what my family said about the dictatorship of Stalin was true. . . . I do not know how to change my soul for the fourth time. . . . I have no basis for believing anything.

Such an experience can hardly fail to make an individual cynical or apathetic. He avoids taking sides or positions of responsibility; he will not be caught napping again. Such attitudes are especially common in countries which have gone through the experience of totalitarianism and its aftermath of nazification and denazification, of purges and counterpurges. But the problem is an even more general one, connected with the phenomenon of "depolitization." The less the chance of the individual in a mass society to control events, the lower his political *and* his ideological concern, and—in an endless and vicious circle—the more frantic the ideological appeals of those actual or would-be rulers who feel the need for ever more fervent adherence. For totalitarian regimes this means increasing difficulty in binding the ruled indefinitely to their control. In its turn, democracy has to steer the difficult path between political apathy, creating what the French call *incivisme,* and the ever-present totalitarian temptations.

CHURCH AND STATE

Consideration of the role of ideologies in the modern political world inevitably brings us to the problem of the relation between church and state. While political science cannot presume to pass on the ultimate validity of religious truth, it can and indeed must recognize the existence of individual religious beliefs as objective facts and of organized religion as a socially and politically relevant institution. Needless to say, it is the political consequences of both individual belief and organized religion which are our proper concern here.

We may usefully return to the phenomenon of *anomie,* the lack of values of the individual in mass society, to understand the role religion plays in a modern nation and, in particular, the problems created by the sometimes conflicting demands of churches and the modern state. Industrialization, urbanization, and the resulting mechanization of life have confronted religion with new tasks which it can shun only at the risk of becoming a mere "Sunday creed," without vital commitment to, and connection with, modern life. If, in the past, religion served the social function of transmitting from generation to generation the generally accepted values, it can today assume the function of providing individuals who are lost in a directionless maze with new or new-old standards, and thereby give direction and meaning to the lives of many who have failed to develop their own.

In assuming this responsibility, however, different religions may follow different paths, and it is important, in relating them to the state and to politics, to understand these differences. Protestantism, for instance, turns primarily to the individual and asks him to turn to the word of God and interpret and live up to it on his own responsibility. Catholicism, with its belief in the Church as the divine organization for guiding its members, confronts both the individual and the polity with fixed standards and established demands. It is, therefore, not surprising that conflicts, wherever they arise between the secular and the spiritual, the law and policy of the state and the creed and dogma of religion, tend to become more conspicuous and sometimes more violent when the more tightly organized churches are involved. In the modern world, it is Roman Catholicism and, possibly, Islam, rather than Protestantism or Buddhism or the Orthodox Church in Russia, which stand up to secularism with the coherent and unified power of a "living faith." And since the Catholic Church and the Moslem religion still have a powerful hold over the people of many countries and regions of the world, the issues in which state and religion are opposed are often most clear-cut where these two religions are involved. For example, the states where the relation between public and religiously controlled education is most difficult—France, Germany, and Italy—are precisely those states where Christian Democratic, i.e., strongly Catholic, parties feel deeply on this issue.

The issue of education, however, is only one among many over which state and church have been divided in modern times. There may be conflicts over the claim of secular power to participate in appointments to clerical office, in particular where the clergy, in turn, participates in civil matters like education or administering marriage contracts; over the church's claim to have the sole right to administer such contracts, or to have its view prevail in matters of family law (divorce) or criminal law (abortion, euthanasia), or such matters of more general and increasingly serious concern as family planning and birth control; or to pass on, if not exercise censorship over, publications and other channels and media of communication. And it is by no means only in relation to the Catholic Church that such conflicts may arise. Any similarly comprehensive belief system is likely to get involved in conflicts. Orthodox Judaism, for example, is represented in Israel through its own political parties, which, if they were able to do so, would force their own Sabbath and dietary laws on orthodox and non-orthodox alike; as it is, they have been able to prevent the adoption of a modern family law. So it is also with Islam in Pakistan and the Middle East, where it has or seeks predominant influence. And so it is to a considerable degree with the Dutch Reformed Church in South Africa—with its rigid Calvinism and strong "elitist" and authoritarian overtones.

In understanding the issues and conflicts that may arise, however, we must distinguish among three types of situations: (1) where there is an established or an actually dominant church; (2) where there is either complete separation between church and state or where there is separation in principle and the churches have certain defined privileges; and (3) where religion faces its most powerful modern opponent, totalitarianism.

State Relations with a Dominant Church

There are still a good many states where the dominance of one religion and one church is accepted and where the church, the government, and the general life and society of the country are closely connected. This situation, of course, reflects the premodern historical relationship between church and state, in which the church, particularly through its control of education and its influence on the prevailing moral and spiritual atmosphere in the country, in effect provided the ideological foundation of the political regime. Frequently, too, the church was related socially and economically with the regime either through ownership of land or because important state positions were held by members of the clergy. The church could then be identified with the *status quo* by both adherents and opponents of the clergy. To opponents it might become, as did the French church, Voltaire's *"l'infâme,"* an institution to be crushed by a violently anticlerical and, quite possibly, antireligious revolution. But such a revolution, on the other hand, could appear to many people as destructive of the moral foundations of a country and thus would rally against it not only the defenders of the old regime but all those fearful of atheism, laicism, and similar tendencies. As we have seen in Spain and Mexico in this century, in such a conflict the issue of the power and influence of the church can become enmeshed with all the other great issues of ideology and politics which divide a nation.

There are many modern states in which such close ties exist. The Ethiopian Constitution of 1955, for instance, declares the Orthodox Church the established church of the state. Pakistan calls itself an "Islamic Republic." In India, the Hindu Mahasabha made a strong though unsuccessful bid to establish Hinduism as the official religious basis of the new polity. Even in Israel, Jewish law is still part of the secular code. It is Catholicism, however, which provides perhaps the most significant case in point, in view of the large number of countries, especially in Latin America, which maintain a close connection between the state and the Catholic Church. In Colombia, for example, the Roman Catholic religion is established as "the official religion of the nation under the protection of the public powers."

Spain may serve as an illustration of the problems and difficulties that can arise under such a system. The Franco regime, actively allied with Catholicism in the Civil War, recognized the Catholic religion as "the religion of the Spanish state [which] will be given official protection" (Article 6 of Franco's "Spaniards' Charter" of 1945), while Article I of the Succession Law of 1947 establishes Spain as "a Catholic, social, and representative State which . . . constitutes a Kingdom." While thus far Spain is a kingdom without a king whose genuinely social and representative character may be in doubt, there can be no question about the role that the Church (together with the army and the Falange) has played as one of the three pillars of the regime. What unites Franco and the Church is above all a common fear of an anti-Franco revolution, which, whether liberal, socialist, or Communist, would threaten the Church with a loss of the prerogatives it considers vital.

It is perhaps the more significant that despite this common interest and the predominant Catholicism of the Spanish people, there have been conflicts between the state and the Church. Thus Franco was unwilling to grant the full measure of the Church's claim to internal organizational autonomy; and in his Concordat with the Vatican (1953) he reserved to the state quite far-reaching rights over appointments to high clerical office. Moreover, in the contested issue of secondary education, with its system of parallel public and religious schools, the Church has had to grant the state supervision over its educational system. On the other hand, the Spanish clergy has frequently criticized some of the more repressive policies of the political regime, in particular its suppression of labor demands and its lack of concern for the living conditions of the poor, since these directly challenge the social tenets of the Church. It is worth noting that failure to take note of such conditions has in the past alienated large classes from organized religion.

Separation of State and Church

If issues between public power and organized religion arise even where there is an official church, it is hardly surprising that they may become even more acute where such a connection does not exist. Usually, the least ground for conflict is found where, as in Anglo-Saxon societies, separation prevails on the basis of mutual toleration and mutual freedom in the vital field of education. This presupposes a meeting of minds or of basic value standards—as in Britain between the general public spirit and the Anglican as well as the nonconformist creeds, and in the United States between the spirit of the public schools and that of the private, including the Catholic, parochial establishments. In the case of America, the potential gap between Christian tenets and the objectives of a competitive society has been bridged by a common acceptance of a set of values and ideals which are indicated in the necessarily somewhat vague term "the American way of life."

But where, as in most Continental European countries, either disestablishment has taken place against the opposition of the churches, or where the churches, although not recognized as official, enjoy certain privileges, we frequently encounter a conflict situation. The issue then tends to oppose the religious side to "laicism," which rejects such privileges and opposes any attempt on the part of the disestablished churches to regain their former privileges. Such a conflict may result in antireligious discrimination, and churches may be deprived not only of their former privileges, but also of the rights they would customarily enjoy even under a system of complete separation. On the other hand, a grant of privileges, such as the right to control education either through a system of church-run schools or through public schools in which instruction proceeds in the spirit of the respective denomination, might tie the church so closely to secular authority that religion assumes an almost official character; this is especially the case where churches are subsidized by the state. Thus, in the Protestant regions of Germany, religion has been so closely tied to the state that the pastor functioned, and still tends to be considered, as part of the state bureaucracy. In France, on the other hand, where "laicization" was enforced upon the religious part of the population, the antagonism of state and church perpetuates itself even to this day on the local and personal level in the relations between priest and (laicist) school teacher; the same is true in parts of Italy. In either case, the issue can become one of the most profound ones dividing a nation, especially where it leads to the formation of Christian or Catholic parties or other parties whose platforms are characterized by their stand on the religious issue. Matters are made worse when the schism is accompanied by division in nationality or language groups. Thus, in Belgium, where the Flemish are more religious than the Walloon part of the population, a conflict over the education of teachers and state subsidies for the denominational school system not only involved the Social Christian Party in a struggle with the Liberal and Socialist Parties, but resulted in reviving the old and bitter antagonism between the two population groups.

Wherever the law of the state decides issues in a way irreconcilable with religious tenets, individuals may find themselves in agonizing conflicts of conscience. The most obvious example is the conscientious objector who will go to prison rather than bear arms. But large-scale passive or even active resistance to the state authority may arise if national policies clash with the standards of a group which holds a nonconforming supranational creed or ideology. Democratic states are usually too tolerant and too responsive to the pressures of particular groups to permit public policy drastically to violate individual or group consciences. But such conflicts can easily arise between religion and a totalitarian regime.

Churches and Totalitarian Regimes

In the past, churches, as one of the famous two pillars of feudal-monarchical rule—"throne and altar"—have often endorsed established social groups and conservative political forces. This made them suspect to reformers, and especially to socialists, as dispensers of "quietism" who, in Marx's phrase, purvey a spiritual opium to the ruled to keep them in an obedient frame of mind. Those who became alienated from religion for this reason often subsequently turned against churches and religion as such, especially if they themselves attained political power. The churches, in turn, tended to consider "atheistic Communism" their chief political enemy. When totalitarian movements rose to power under anti-Communist slogans, religious groups were therefore tempted to align themselves with these movements as allies in a common cause. This was clearest in the case of Spanish Falangism; but even in the case of Nazism, major portions of German Protestantism at first welcomed Hitler, and the Vatican concluded a Concordat with him in 1933 (as it had done earlier with Mussolini) in the hope of mutual accommodation.

Usually, however, it has not taken long to persuade churches and religions that, short of sacrificing their own fundamental interests and beliefs, they cannot hope to come to terms, and even less to make common cause, with any kind of totalitarianism that takes its own ideology seriously. Both Protestantism and Catholicism ended in violent conflict with Nazism in Germany; conflict with the Church arose irrepressibly even in a Catholic country like Argentina under Peron; and as we have seen, church and state are not free from tension in Franco Spain. Religion and fascist totalitarianism (in the broader sense of the term) are incompatible, because they represent rival and total ideological claims. Even where fascism does not profess hostility to religion, it is so fundamentally wedded to ideals and principles which Christianity abhors that any real conciliation is impossible. Mussolini's ideal of bellicism and the warlike virtues, his glorification of integral nationalism as an end, and of force, violence, terror, cunning—in short, all the

Machiavellian devices—as proper means, were no less pagan than Hitler's racialism and all that it involved. In South Africa, with the increasingly oppressive racialism of the regime, the churches are in a quandary, and even where they, or prominent church leaders, enunciate a liberal view on race relations, their words and example appear to have little general effect.

Communism is no less fundamentally opposed to religious tenets than fascism, since it, too, demands the complete allegiance of its members. Thus the church-state conflict in Catholic countries under satellite rule has been inevitable. Moreover, Christian parties have been in the vanguard of anti-Communist coalitions and policies in the postwar period, and in Italy, they constitute *the* one big non-Communist party. A 1949 decree by the Congregation of the Holy Office in Rome declared that any association of a Catholic with the Communist Party, either as a member or in other ways, or through any activity in support of Communist doctrine and practice was forbidden and would incur automatic excommunication.

Can there ever be a *rapprochement* or even a *modus vivendi* between organized religion and Communism? At this point, the prospects of an accommodation on any other basis than an uneasy truce, in which churches avoid overly harsh criticism of the regime and the regime avoids harsh persecution of the churches, seem rather dim. But the argument has sometimes been made that while fascism is pagan, Communism is rather a "Christian heresy." This line of thought holds that the ultimate ideal of Marxian socialism, which Communism still professes, is not entirely incompatible with religious ethics: it is humanitarian and even personalistic, concerned with individuals and a better life rather than with the glory and power of nations or races, or the power of an elite or a *Fuehrer*.

Communism, especially during the Stalin era, perverted these ideals. And while, as we have seen, changes in the post-

Stalin era have softened the conflict to some extent, they have not yet gone far enough, at least in the Soviet Union, to proffer much hope for a reversal so profound as to bring the professed ideal into accord with practice. In a Communist country such as Poland, on the other hand, there is, perhaps, somewhat more ground for hope that Communism may change more fundamentally. Should this happen, and Communism, or at least one of its versions, gradually develop in such a way as to shed its most totalitarian features, including repressive policies vis-à-vis churches and religion, an accommodation might then conceivably become possible. Churches have proved themselves adaptable to a wide variety of situations without sacrificing their ultimate goals; they have been able to cross the divide between continents, races, and civilizations; and they have been wont to take the long-range view, especially when the fate of many of their members was at stake. For the time being, however, their interests as well as their ideals are more intimately connected with the liberal-democratic polities.

The Liberal and the Totalitarian Polity

For the time being, Communism remains the challenge to religion as well as to the democracies. In view of this fact, the latter will naturally ally themselves with forces and movements opposed to any form of totalitarianism: with churches and religions as long as they do not support fascist regimes or trends, and also with those governments which, while not completely democratic according to the exacting standards of the older Western democracies, yet recognize some necessary restraints and limitations upon power in order to protect individual and group rights and liberties. Some of these latter governments, because of their authoritarian heritage, have failed thus far to live up fully to all the criteria established by British or American democracy. This is still true of Germany and likewise of Japan, whose modern political developments resemble those of Germany in so many respects and whose late industrialization and strong authoritarian traditions have so far hampered genuine democratization. Not all modernized countries have been fortunate enough to enjoy the steady growth over several centuries of that incubator of liberal and democratic institutions, a rising middle class. And the newly independent countries of Asia, Africa, and the Middle East have had an even more sudden break with the past.

Recognizing the existence of such handicaps to democratic development, those nations committed to democracy can profitably draw the distinction between political democracy and liberalism which we have previously suggested, and welcome as allies in the antitotalitarian camp nations and regimes which, while more or less authoritarian in their political institutions or in their approach to decision-making, are yet liberal in the sense of respecting and protecting the dignity of the individual and the free expression of personal and group interests. As the Central European *Rechtsstaat* shows, this combination is a practicable one. In other words, where traditionalism does not exclude individual freedom and the development of personality, it may constitute a bulwark against totalitarian inroads.

This distinction between authoritarianism and totalitarianism may possibly also become a reality should a part of the Communist world develop a system in which individuals and private groups will be granted substantial and reliable protection of basic liberties, even though the ruling group and party do not give up their decision-making controls. It is too early at this point to venture predictions as to when and where this might happen, but if one or the other of the former East European satellites of the Soviet Union, or even the U.S.S.R. itself, should enter upon this path, Western democracy would no longer have to consider such a regime its "natural enemy."

An ideology of anti-Communism that for doctrinal reasons should fail or refuse to take notice of such developments and transformations in the opposite camp would be as dangerous as a dogmatic totalitarianism of the Communist variety. But as long as the dogmatic approach continues to hold its own in at least part of the Communist camp—and there are indications that the Sino-Soviet split not only reflects but tends to keep the Chinese and their followers in the area of full-fledged and "unreconstructed" totalitarianism—there is, of course, no reason to discontinue the opposition which the liberal democracies must offer to what is in essence hostile to its basic values.

Thus, in distinguishing between dictatorship and democracy, or totalitarianism and liberalism, what counts even more than the rule, or absence of the rule, of the majority is the right, or at least the reasonable chance, for individuals and associations of individuals freely to develop themselves. Particularly in our mass societies, where the people can exercise at best only a limited control over crucial matters of domestic and foreign policy, the difference between free and totalitarian countries seems to reduce itself ultimately to one question: whether or not there exists an inviolable sphere of privacy in which the otherwise organized, mechanized, ordered, and oftentimes bullied individual may yet proceed according to his will, whim, or fantasy, his beliefs or disbeliefs, in a socially useful and adjusted or an entirely useless and unadjusted fashion. Any genuine freedom in the personal and group spheres presupposes, as we have seen, the placing of limits upon political power. It is only when there are limits on what government may do and on the way in which it may do it that citizens are free. Thus, if religion may be an ally of democracy in its conflict with totalitarianism, liberal democracy, in turn, provides the setting within which a man can most freely maintain those beliefs, religious or secular, which enhance his individuality.

VIII

THE INTERRELATIONS
OF NATIONAL AND
INTERNATIONAL POLITICS

No less intimately interrelated than belief systems and politics are national and international affairs. A major trend of recent times has been the growing interdependence and integration of nations in an international system where many of them become ever less independent of foreign influence and none can escape the impact of growing world integration. Although the number of formally and legally "independent" states has increased rapidly over the last two decades, they and all others tend to be grouped into a relatively few large blocs. And while technologically, economically, and otherwise all are coming closer to each other on a shrinking globe, at the same time, and paradoxically, they are ever more deeply divided into politically, ideologically, and oftentimes emotionally antagonistic groupings.

The impact of this dual development is reflected not only in the foreign, but increasingly also in the domestic affairs of even the largest and most powerful nations; it must be analyzed with care if the study of government is to be both perceptive and genuinely comparative.

FROM SELF-SUFFICIENCY TO INTERDEPENDENCE

It is not without reason that students of comparative government have long ignored, or paid scant attention to, the impact of international affairs on national governments and politics. For some three or more centuries after the modern nation-state emerged in the late fifteenth and early sixteenth centuries, domestic affairs were relatively autonomous. Political institutions grew out of native soil, and changes, even revolutionary ones, were due to indigenous forces and indigenous movements. Foreign influences were not themselves without effect; but they were commonly transformed and shaped to fit the needs of the respective nation. Thus, liberal democracy, as we have seen, would change in coloring or even in meaning when exported from one environment to another. Indeed, throughout this period, domestic political forces and movements were less influenced by foreign affairs than themselves influences on foreign policies, as, for example, when Britain or the United States sided with liberal democratic forces or nations, or Czarist Russia backed the cause of absolutism on the Continent for its own internal political reasons.

Domestic considerations, of course, are still powerful in the policies of nations, and especially in those which retain the largest measure of freedom of movement in their foreign affairs. But, by and large, our era is noteworthy for the increase in the impact which world affairs have on internal politics and institutions. One main reason for this change lies in the transformation of the nature and function of the nation-state itself: its transformation, that is, from a fortress into an entity incapable of assured defense against modern weapons of attack.

The essential characteristic of the modern territorial state used to be that it was a self-contained, closed, centralized unit which could provide its citizens with protection, both in the form of internal peace and of security from outside control or interference. Fortresses lining its boundaries rendered it difficult even for stronger countries to penetrate by force of arms; and security was strengthened by alliances of weaker powers with stronger ones, by nations' interest in the maintenance of a balance of power, and, prior to the French Revolution, by a feeling among rulers that "legitimate" units as such should not be destroyed. Subsequently, when dynastic legitimacy yielded to national self-determination, the national units acquired a cohesion which made them even more integrated and permitted internal government and constitutional life to develop in accordance with the indigenous trends and inclinations of the nation's people.

By the end of the last century, however, certain developments presaged the end of this system. With industrialization, economic self-sufficiency became transformed into dependence on continued imports from abroad. World War I showed how close both Britain and Germany could come to defeat through blockade. But the decisive change has been in the nature of war. Air war, by opening the way to "vertical" invasion, has meant the end of the frontier in its traditional function of protection. Thus the basic condition which gave substance to legal sovereignty and political independence came to an end, and with it the sense of security which had enabled countries to develop their own political institutions and ways of life. To this feeling of insecurity, the possibility of a sudden, unannounced, annihilating blow by nuclear weapons now adds a sense of complete impotence. Even the nuclear powers not only possess the overwhelming power to inflict absolute destruction on others, but, like the non-nuclear powers, are themselves equally exposed to destruction.

Although it is clear that the sense of security and protection which the traditional nation-state provided cannot be restored under nuclear conditions short of a world-state with nuclear monopoly, few people, and even few leaders, have grasped the radical nature of this change from relative self-sufficiency to interdependence. In the main, states have continued to act as if they were still the sovereign independent units of the past. The chief difference was that, in the postwar period, their efforts were directed at pushing the wall of protection, which had surrounded individual nations, farther out, so that it now would encircle entire continents and thus comprise groups of nations. This effort, undertaken in order to gain that security which is no longer attainable within national boundaries, started at the two centers of power that had emerged from World War II: the United States and the Soviet Union. It thus led to the phenomenon of "bipolarity"—that is, the formation of the two blocs, East and West—whose antagonism, accentuated by the ideological conflict between Communism and democracy, lent its imprint to the Cold War of that period. The leading, or "super"-powers in each camp have tried to bring ever more countries under their influence, or at least to deny them, ideologically, politically, and economically, to the other side.

More recently fissures have appeared on either side. With the development of China and the Sino-Soviet split, and the growing inclination of "satellites" and "allies" to reassert themselves (such as Gaullism in the Western camp), some observers have foreseen the end of bipolarity and the rise of a new nuclear system of multipolarity. It seems, however, that for the time being, the two leading powers are still dominant. What then has been the impact of their predominance on the government and politics of their own and other nations?

THE IMPACT OF BIPOLARITY

Bipolarity has had two chief effects. One is that domestic issues have tended to recede before foreign affairs. The other is that the leading powers and their policies have exercised more and more influence not only on the foreign, but also on the domestic affairs of other countries.

The first effect is perhaps more noticeable in democracies than in totalitarian countries. The functioning of liberal democracy has always been favored by the existence of peace, or at least of that "normalcy" in which wars were rare enough not to disturb their institutions radically and limited enough not to affect an underlying feeling of security. But since World War I in Europe, and since the end of World War II in America, too, crisis conditions in international affairs have almost become the normal ones; we are perennially involved in cold wars and even relieved when an outbreak of actual hostilities leads merely to localized conflict instead of the dread total war. Clearly, this situation favors authoritarianism over democratic institutions; concentration of power (especially in the executive, if not the military) rather than its limitation or dispersion; broad and ill-defined mandates rather than checks and controls; and restrictions or suspensions of individual or group rights rather than their jealous protection.

The Effect of Emergencies, Actual and Potential

The bipolar split and the threat of nuclear annihilation have not, however, had the same far-reaching impact in all places and at all times. It differs in different nations and tends to change with the ups and downs in the Cold War (or "cold peace") situation. Thus, at times the West has been more concerned with the economic offensive of the Eastern bloc than with threats of actual hostilities. At other times, however, the threat of Soviet, and more recently Chinese, penetration into vital areas of Africa, the Middle East, Southeast Asia, and (with Cuba) even the Western hemisphere, has deeply affected American as well as West European policies.

Such ups and downs should not deceive us into believing that, as in former ages, emergencies will come and go. The threat that nuclear war poses is a continual one, and the emergency is thus potentially always with us. We may hope that the "balance of terror"—the nuclear stalemate between the two blocs—will ensure permanent peace, but we cannot depend on it. Crises are apt to recur; and while totalitarian regimes, with their concentration of power and their absence of checks and limitations, are prepared in any case to meet crises, even where they do not provoke them, democracies, if they would try to preserve their traditional values and institutions, are confronted with grave difficulties.

These dangers were illustrated by what happened in the United States at the height of the Cold War. That threats to national security may give rise to emotionalism or even to hysteria (however that loosely used term may be defined) had already been shown by the American Alien and Sedition Acts of the Napoleonic period. But the threat to traditional liberties, indeed to established constitutional life, has become even greater in our nuclear, bipolar age. The power of investigation with all its connotations and effects—a power which for a while was almost unlimited and unchecked—not only affected rights and liberties (the sphere that attracted most attention), but also such constitutional principles as the separation of powers in government itself. Thus it threatened at one point to render lower and intermediate levels of the executive subject to control by members of the Congress, thereby undermining the hierarchy of the executive and the authority of its chief. And it is significant that it was neither the chief executive nor the broad public revulsion to which "McCarthyism" eventually yielded. Its decline was due rather to the fact that a recession in international tension coincided with resistance on the part of smaller groups, in particular the Federal judiciary and the leaders in the Protestant churches and in some universities. As for the Senator's personal power, it was a tradition-minded group of his colleagues which was chiefly responsible for its decline.

Discouraging as much of this experience was, it also demonstrated that democracy has a resilience under stress which asserts itself sometimes in unexpected ways. Likewise, it tended to show that it is less the constitutional framework that lends or denies protection to national institutions than it is the traditions of nations and the spirit in which they and their leaders act. This can be seen still better from the way in which West European nations reacted to the Cold War situation. Thus the British, whose government had made a cautious and restrained use of legally unlimited emergency powers in both world wars, proved similarly sober in their approach to postwar problems of internal security. Instead of flooding the country with loyalty investigations and subjecting the entire civil service to uniform security standards, they applied these to carefully selected sensitive agencies and only to positions where spies or subversives might do real damage. More important, they never yielded to the frenzy of fear and suspicion which leads to the invasion of vital personal concerns with far-fetched charges, "faceless" accusers, and ostracism. This experience would seem to indicate that, difficult as is the problem posed to democracies by a permanent emergency in world relations, sacrifice of liberties is not inevitable.

But because McCarthyism has come and gone, we should not for this reason underestimate the less spectacular but more lasting effects of potential emergencies. Americans in particular are wont to personalize politics and thus, in this instance, to think of McCarthy as *the* danger (or the hero, as the case may be). But the trends are still there; so are the instruments. Thus, an Act of 1950 grants the President sweeping emergency powers, which may be invoked on his finding that "an attack upon the United States has occurred or is anticipated"; in this instance, he may even detain suspect persons in concentration camps.

One of the most important needs of a democracy is a constant, unimpeded flow of information. Here, too, world tension is taking its toll. Withholding information for security reasons was intensified with the advent of "atomic secrets"; more and more government activities, moreover, are now "classified," thus all too often limiting information to predigested official news handouts. To some degree this is inevitable. Who among the uninitiated can judge the requirements for defense and defense establishments and their related budgetary and other legislation? Who can judge what measures are best fitted to counter an alleged or a real aggression? But if active citizenship is not to be excluded from the fields of defense and foreign affairs, such a development means that responsible leaders have still greater need than in the past to keep the public informed not only of the reasons for such limits on information, but also of the basis on which the judgments in these fields are made.

This is no less true with respect to another effect of the nuclear age: the fact that dependence on nuclear weapons may render necessary quick decisions of a vital character. These decisions, in the ultimate case, can hardly be arrived at through prolonged democratic discussion of issues. And the ultimate decisions may be prejudiced by preceding foreign policies or, perhaps even more, by preceding military policies, which in turn may have been arrived at without genuine democratic participation or consent. Thus the procedures of democracy tend to be limited to less vital areas, and a still greater importance is placed on the responsibility of its leaders.

The Trend Toward Conformity

We should also notice one further effect of bipolarity: what may be called the "neutralization" of politics, the trend toward avoiding strong attitudes for or against this or that policy. Bipolarity, which implies ideological cleavage, tends to render unpopular or even unusual attitudes, whether held by individuals or by groups, suspect. This has always been a characteristic of totalitarianism, where the essence of control consists in the suppression of deviating opinion. But it is becoming noticeable in nontotalitarian countries also. The very existence of a totalitarian opponent tends to render dissent suspect, and thus to encourage conformity. But, strangely, such conformity does not reject what Communism, where it is in actual control, stands for: authoritarianism, rigidity, deprivation of liberty. On the contrary, conformity opposes what Communism itself destroys: espousal of reform, protection of rights, safeguarding of liberties. This renders the less stout citizen timid; for fear of being tainted "red" he tries hard to appear colorless and to avoid the controversial. While in the nineteenth century broad movements for change and reform in the major nations were often backed by large popular majorities, today most of the people in some of the same countries are either politically apathetic or conservative (if not reactionary). While in the last century young people, and especially university students, were in the forefront of reform, today it is rather the small elite groups which retain interest in the great political issues. Opinion studies of the 1950's reveal how small a percentage of the average people in the United States, for instance, stood for protection of civil liberties; and in Germany, the flight into political neutrality characterizes even groups which, like labor, used to be in the forefront of political action. Only recently have larger numbers of people, and in particular students and clergymen, taken renewed interest in world affairs and assumed an active role in issues such as the civil and political rights of Negroes in the United States.

Other factors besides bipolarization have helped to create a trend toward conformity. The making and taking of vital decisions without the participation of the public, which lacks the necessary information for reasons we have noted, cannot help but create political indifference. There is the impact of the mass media of communication, which tend to devote little time and effort to political matters, and, when they do handle them, tend to be rather colorless. Lastly, the rising living standard and improved social services in countries like the United States and Britain, by wiping out a good deal of the former inequities in wealth or status, have rendered large numbers of people so satisfied that their interest in class or other social and economic issues has declined.

On the other hand, it is in countries and regions like Latin America, the Middle East, the Far East, or Southeast Asia that the political involvement and concern which we characterized as typical of the nineteenth century still prevail. It is noteworthy that it is in just these areas that student involvement in politics is still common, as witness the role of students in the 1960 overthrow of regimes in Turkey and in Korea.

We thus arrive at the somewhat paradoxical conclusion that although grinding poverty, economic anxiety, or class division render the functioning of genuine democracy difficult, the very solution of these problems likewise involves difficulties to democracy. Can a society which has reached a high level of material satisfaction generate that continual concern with civic issues that is at the root of active democracy? Can it do so particularly in times when concern with domestic matters is bound periodically to recede behind apprehensions about the international situation?

Relations Between Stronger and Lesser Powers

Let us now turn to the other impact of the new power system in the world, that of the superpowers on lesser states and, in particular, on their allies. There is nothing new in unequal relationships between stronger and weaker powers. They have, in the past, accounted for dependencies of all sorts, ranging all the way from mere strategic or economic influences to protectorate or colonial relationships. But except in the latter case, when the dominant power assumes complete control, domestic affairs have usually stayed within the autonomous control of the weaker power. The contrast today is that similar relations tend to affect to a greater degree the internal policies and systems of the dependent units. This does not mean that such dependency automatically involves control over the details of day-to-day policy-making. But it may well affect a nation's fundamental decisions about social and economic structure, political constitutions and freedoms, and similar basic issues, which used to be settled through the actions of national parties or movements within the framework of national institutions and processes.

The issue of internal Communism is the most striking example of this trend. The Communist Party is still legal and still strong in France and in Italy. But it is practically excluded from official positions in government coalitions. This is because internal alignments in our day are liable to have foreign-policy connotations. As long as Italy is in NATO, for instance, can one visualize Communist participation in a government through which Communist ministers might share the secrets of a military alliance? The Communist Party, as ex-Premier Mollet has put it, is "neither Left nor Right, but East."

In the East, of course, anything other than Communism is excluded. But Western democratic states have also tried, from time to time, to make use of their influence in order to ensure what might be called the stability, "political health," or reliability of an ally. What happened in Athens at the time of "liberation" at the end of World War II (as reported by Churchill) differed little even in detail from what happened at the same time in Bucharest. In the 1950's, the United States twice interfered in Greece in order to influence a change in its electoral system, not because it feared that the existing system might result in the victory of what was, in any case, an outlawed Communist Party, but in order to enhance the chances of a group of parties believed to be more favorably inclined to the West than was another group. There was open use of American influence on behalf of the Christian Democrats at the time of the Italian election of 1953. In the same year, American backing of Adenauer and his Christian Democrats in West Germany was not without effect on his victory over the Social Democrats, who were likewise Western-oriented but at that time still somewhat neutralist. The possibility of an "agonizing reappraisal" of American policy was made known to a France hesitant to integrate itself with Europe, and particularly with Western Germany. At that time, a French journalist was said to have declared that he would now take out American citizenship papers so as to be able to exercise some influence on French affairs! And what, at times, is the so-called Johnson Doctrine other than the claimed right of the United States to intervene in Latin American countries whenever in its judgment there is the threat of a Communist take-over?

But, as the Dominican case shows, attempts to influence too closely or too rudely the affairs of less powerful countries are apt to backfire. This is why, more recently, the influence exercised by the superpowers over their allies has lessened somewhat, or at least, been commonly more subtle and indirect. This trend has been in reaction to the tendency on the part of these allies to assert their autonomy or independence more forcefully. Even Soviet control of "satellite" affairs, formerly exercised primarily through Soviet Army and Communist Party control over the respective governments, encountered resistance and "national deviation" and has since lessened to such an extent that it can hardly be compared any more to the dependency relationship that prevailed under Stalin. However, the basic decision in favor of a Communist type of economy, society, and government is still not an indigenous one. The Hungarian Revolution and its defeat showed clearly the limits set to the freedom of action of the non-Soviet members of the Soviet bloc.

In the West, interference of the type mentioned above has likewise become rarer. But the over-all issue of foreign-policy "orientation," in this case of Western orientation, still has its impact on internal policies and alignments. This issue tends either to make any but the alliance orientation appear subversive and thus compel all major groups and parties to agree basically on one and the same foreign policy; or it may tend to split all or most of the existing groups and parties over this issue. In the latter event, a Western orientation may raise more political and general antagonism than it is worth militarily; it may even lead, as in Iceland or Morocco, to the threatened denunciation of arrangements for the stationing of troops or airbases. This will then confront the "occupying" power with the choice of trying to hold on by force or of yielding to circumstances, the more common reaction.

Such foreign- or military-policy issues tend in many of the lesser powers to overshadow what used to be considered the more vital domestic issues: those of socialism, the welfare state, or free enterprise. Thus, whereas parties and movements were seldom divided primarily over foreign affairs in the past, these issues now have so great an impact on the lesser powers that questions like neutralism vs. alignment with a superpower, the granting of bases to a foreign power, colonialism, imperialism, and the like often preoccupy their minds and policies to the exclusion, or at least the detriment, of internal issues. This cannot fail to have its effect on traditional party systems and policies. With the exception of the Communist Party and, to a lesser extent, the MRP (Mouvement Républicain Populaire), there was not a single French party which was not split about equally over the issue of the European Defense Community. In West Germany, the effect has been the opposite—one of leading almost every party to agree on the basic, that is, the Western, foreign-policy orientation. In Britain, the two great parties are basically bipartisan on foreign issues (their sharp differences over British military action during the Suez crisis were almost without precedent), so that where there is some opposition to current foreign policy, as, for example, over the question of nu-

clear armaments, it cuts into a particular party, such as the Labour Party, and weakens it from within. Thus the international
situation influences the relations, alignments, and strength of
those political forces within nations which used to be guided
primarily by domestic issues.

The Major Powers and the "Uncommitted" World

Lastly, we may ask how bipolarity with its ascendancy of the
superpowers has affected those nations which so far have
avoided close alignment with either bloc, and in this sense are
uncommitted. For the most part, the latter belong to the category of underdeveloped or "developing" countries. Many of
them are newly independent and thus faced with the problems
of establishing their own political and constitutional systems
and procedures. In many of them, such as India, Nigeria, or the
Philippines, previous Western influence and control have determined their present governmental institutions and political
processes at least in a formal way. Western-type parliamentary
systems, parties, and elections abound; and occasionally the experience of these nations has added significantly to our knowledge of democratic possibilities, as when elections in India and
Nigeria demonstrate that literacy is not an indispensable re-
quirement for genuine expression of the popular will. Whether
or not these countries become genuine democracies depends,
however, both on their own evolving traditions and on the influence and example of the major powers.

Let us consider for a moment some of the pulls and counterpulls which operate on such underdeveloped but steadily
advancing states. Since they have only recently evolved from colonial status and have done so mainly as the result of nationalist
movements which demanded independence, these states are
anticolonial in attitude. The very fact that the powers from
which they gained their independence were Western ones can,
though not necessarily does, provide a natural bias against the

latter, which the Soviet Union or China can try to exploit. Moreover, because Western countries have a relatively high standard of living, their experience may well seem to have less relevance to developing countries than that of a state like the Soviet Union or more particularly China, which so recently was in a condition like their own.

It would be a mistake to underestimate, however, the attraction of the liberal democratic ideal to some of these newly emancipated states. It may well be true that to the great mass of their people it is more important to escape from their grinding poverty than to secure personal liberties. But even the most poverty-stricken person has a sense of his own personal dignity for which he desires respect. Even at this level the right to protest and to propose is a cherished one. But more important in shaping the immediate destinies of states like India and Nigeria is the fact that their leaders have a keen feeling for democratic values and are attempting courageously in the face of great difficulties to put them into operation in their societies.

Seen in this context, it is not what the Western democracies say in the way of propaganda that will be decisive for their influence in the uncommitted countries, but what they do. The action (or inaction) of the Western powers will be significant on two quite different levels. In the first place, it is obvious that their activities can have a great impact when they answer the basic needs of these countries. There are two ways in which the developing nations can modernize and industrialize: through their own unaided efforts but at the cost of totalitarian controls such as those of the Soviet Union or Communist China, or with assistance from outside. If it can be shown that Western economic and technical assistance will aid their development to such a degree that they can both modernize themselves and retain their Western-type institutions and freedoms, these institutions may gain the mass backing which is essential for their continued survival. In the competitive struggle with the Communist powers for the good will of these states, it will be far more important to provide this opportunity for democratic institutions to root themselves in popular favor than to achieve any immediate backing on a particular issue.

Not only is it important to provide the kind of economic aid which can underpin democratic regimes; it is also vital for Western states to back up those who struggle to keep them in operation. In this respect, all too little has been done. American ties with Franco Spain can presumably be justified on strategic grounds; but Trujillo's dictatorship in the Dominican Republic received about as much support as its more democratically deserving neighbors. President Jiménez of Venezuela was officially honored in Washington, whereas no similar honor had been conferred on representatives of the preceding democratic regime of that country. When such actions are contrasted with the open American opposition to the leftist (though by no means entirely Communist-controlled) government in Guatemala, which contributed greatly to its overthrow in 1954, or the somewhat comparable revolt in the Dominican Republic in 1965, uncommitted countries may well come to feel that the major Western democratic powers are opposed to only one among many types of nondemocratic governments, or movements. In Africa, American support of Tshombe's Congo regime has given rise to widespread suspicion that business and mining interests are regarded as more important than popular, Pan-Africanist objectives, a view further reinforced by the open and profitable participation of American and British enterprises in the booming white-controlled South African economy.

To support progressive democratic forces in the underdeveloped countries may well be the most, perhaps even the only, effective way to counter potentially strong Soviet or other Communist influence. In its recent policies, the Soviet Union has combined the appeal to indigenous nationalism—the strongest political and ideological force in those areas—with attempts to satisfy these countries' basic material needs through economic aid. In certain respects, its attitude toward these countries has been more "democratic" than that of the democratic states themselves. Thus the Soviet Union has ostentatiously maintained that there are no political strings attached to its economic aid. Moreover, its studied efforts at correctness in its relations with the developing countries sometimes arouse less suspicion than do those of Western countries which still retain vestiges of their traditional attitudes of superiority.

Even more recently than the Soviets, the Communist Chinese have undertaken to extend their influence into the "uncommitted" world, sometimes even opposing Soviet influence as that of a "white" power and in this way have tried to present themselves as the only major people and power that understands the concerns of the colored races and thus is genuinely interested in helping them. Shrewdly exploiting the absence or weakness of an indigenous administrative force in some of the smaller African countries, they have managed to gain strong influence or even control in a selected number of such units (e.g., in Congo Brazzaville), from which they can hope to assist revolutionary groups and movements in neighboring countries (such as Congo Léopoldville). Thus bipolarity, or tripolarity, may affect weaker states in the sense of interference with or even control of their domestic policies and institutions.

In the face of such pressures and allurements, effective democratic influence on the new states also requires a second type of action on the part of Western states: a convincing demonstration that they themselves are truly democratic in actions as well as words. Having long lived under foreign domination and discrimination, the developing countries (or at least their leaders) care as greatly about being treated on a basis of equality and respect as about improving their material conditions. A major reason why the newer countries of the Commonwealth of Nations—India, Pakistan, Ceylon, Ghana, Nigeria, Malaysia, etc.—prize their membership is because, in addition to receiving material advantages, they are treated as equals in that association. To the extent that the West actually practices democratic virtues both in its relations with the new states and at home, it enjoys a vast advantage over its totalitarian opponents, whose words are contradicted by realities, particularly with regard to domestic practices. The degree to which democratic values, especially equality (in particular racial equality) and personal and group liberties, are demonstrable may, in fact, determine in large measure what direction the so-called uncommitted nations will take. Thus the practice of democracy in countries like Great Britain and the United States may turn out to be decisive for the ultimate fate of freedom throughout the world.

THE IMPACT OF INTERNATIONAL ORGANIZATION

We have spoken of the tremendous changes which have transformed a world of self-sufficient and separate nations into an ever more integrated whole within which all nations tend to become interdependent. Population trends and pressures affect not only particular nations, but, with their by-products of migration and (in extreme cases) of refugee and expellee groups and stateless persons, all the other countries, too. The "population explosion" as such (coupled with the exhaustion of vital natural resources and the problem of inadequate food supplies in large parts of the world) poses as great a world problem today as does security from aggression and nuclear annihilation. And as far as the latter is concerned, certainly no more urgent task can be imagined than that of providing for effective collective security or other international devices to protect the world from utter destruction.

And, indeed, there has been no lack of efforts along these lines. For the last hundred years there have been attempts to bring about an ever closer integration of sovereign nations through the establishment of agencies for the pursuit of common purposes. This trend culminated in the League of Nations system and that of its successor, the United Nations, with its many affiliated agencies in economic, cultural, and humanitarian fields. A vast number of activities are now coordinated or carried on through these channels.

The effect of these developments can be interpreted in two very different ways, depending on one's ultimate objective. To those who believe that the effectiveness of international organization depends on the actual transfer of major functions and powers now in the domain of sovereign nations—whether in the fields mentioned above or of security against war and aggression—the progress which has been made is very small. These people would claim that an effective solution of the world-wide problems of resources or of migration requires a transfer of genuine lawmaking powers to a supranational body which would have the power to supervise the implementation of policies and the administration of programs initiated by national agencies. Genuine collective security, in this view, requires the abdication by member nations of discretion over their power to direct military policies and to make war.

In view of the overwhelming common tasks and the equally overwhelming common danger in which mankind finds itself now, and will increasingly find itself in the future, this unification is bound to come some time if the human race is to survive. But it is clear that despite their exposure to nuclear danger and their inability independently to solve other great universal problems, nations have not yet fully grasped this need and thus have been unwilling to make the necessary transfers of jurisdiction and renunciation of power. Whatever they have been doing by way of international cooperation has been (as the term indicates) voluntary and based on calculations of the national interest.

But this is not to say that their interpretation of their vital interests has not led nations to make increasing use of international organization for purposes which are both to their advantage and beyond their own scope. One of the most obvious places where this has happened is in activities which concern refugees: not only in the vast numbers of such homeless people dealt with by the International Refugee Organization through its camps, shipping facilities, and migration service, but also in such sudden emergencies as the one created by the outflow of refugees after the abortive Hungarian revolt against Soviet control in 1956, or in the long-standing situation in which the Palestinian Arabs find themselves. In fields like health, food and agriculture, and technical and economic assistance, international organization is being used to facilitate activities that no one country can adequately undertake on its own. Most spectacular, and ultimately most significant, may be the international forces that maintain the peace between Israel and the Arab states, and did so for some time within the Congo. As a matter of fact, the Congo presented in that period an example of how in the absence of organized internal government, international administrators could take over the functions of such government. As in some previous instances (League of Nations administration of the Saar territory, for instance, or international plebiscite commissions), international organization has proved itself at least technically capable of providing those services which a more nationalistic attitude claims as exclusively national ones.

It would also be a mistake to underestimate the moral and psychological influence of the United Nations. This affects the policies of state both by example and by expectation. The newer countries have learned much about the practices of more mature ones through contact in U.N. organizations. The principle of equality for women and the Declaration of Human Rights may not be accepted fully in some Latin American, Asian, and African countries calling themselves democratic (nor are they accepted as fully in the mature democratic states as they should be), but it becomes more difficult for all these countries to withstand pressures at home to extend such rights when they have been promoted on the international level. From the other side, sensitivity to racial and color discrimination within countries has been greatly intensified through the participation in international agencies of Asians and Africans. Even when nations find justification in traditional standards of self-interest for interfering forcibly in a national situation, as Great Britain and France did in the Suez crisis late in 1956, the protests in the United Nations (and indeed among the British people themselves) indicated new and widespread assumptions about the use of U.N. channels which must inevitably exert an influence on future national policies. Even the Soviet Union, with its rigorous insistence on its right to interfere in the Hungarian uprising and with its vast military strength, had to stand a fire of criticism and moral reprobation from smaller countries, while its efforts to make capital out of the Congo crisis in the early 1960's were largely thwarted through the support of U.N. action by independent African states. In a world where major power blocs strive for the support of the uncommitted countries, debates on the platform of the United Nations are far from being without influence.

For the foreseeable future, it is along these lines that international organization seems likely to have its greatest effect. It is true that here and there, and in a preparatory way, as it were, steps have been taken which might facilitate the working of genuine supranational organization, or even international government, if ever the world should become ready for it. Thus some postwar constitutions, notably those of France and West Germany, and postwar amendments to some older constitutions, notably in the case of Holland and Denmark, provide for a possible transfer of legislative, administrative, and judicial authority to an international organization or organizations.

But the practical significance of the constitutional provisions we have mentioned has not been in relation to international organization in general, but rather with respect to certain regional organizations that have arisen in the postwar period, particularly in Western Europe, such as the European Coal and Steel Community, Euratom, and the Common Market.

These three organizations—which by 1965 were scheduled to be merged into one—have by now coalesced into integrated setups of "supranational" agencies that possess direct powers over individuals and corporations within the constituent nations. In particular, this supranational character applies to the Commission of the Common Market with its far-reaching controls and its own mushrooming staff organization. While the parliament so far has been granted only consultative functions, and the Council of Ministers represents rather the "sovereignty" of the member states, the Commission has grown into the role of representing the "community interest" and the common purpose of all of the Six, and there is even a "constitutional" court watching over the implementation of the common rules.

This new setup may turn out to be of great significance for government and politics in the world to come. Its example may prove that gradual development toward genuine world government is possible through a process of step-by-step devolution of national sovereignty. To be sure, even regional devolution constitutes an extremely complex and at times frustrating process, as witness recent French resistance to more far-reaching steps, and its veto on British entry following earlier British hesitation to join. Both the British and the French attitudes clearly revealed the obstacles posed by national interests and by the traditional disinclination on the part of nationally organized groups such as political parties, or indeed of states themselves to yield the influence they now wield in favor of playing a less certain and less predictable role in the environment of an existing or enlarged regional setup.

In regard to European regionalism, a group like British Labour may have legitimate grounds to fear that it might be unable to pursue policies of nationalization in the European-wide framework which it may be able to put into practice within the national framework of its country. On the other hand, there have been complaints—apparently well-founded—from within the Six that the growing "European" bureaucracy at Brussels has been showing the tendency of all bureaucracy to get snarled in red tape, to extend its influence beyond due limits, and in this way to hamper the legitimate autonomies of the members, their parliaments, and their individual administrations. The De Gaulle veto on British entry into the Common Market demonstrated unwillingness to share control within a regional unit containing so powerful an additional unit. Thus it is only by giving careful consideration to both supranational and national interests and aspirations that regional integration will prove successful over the long pull.

What has developed in Western Europe, however, shows that at least some nations under certain circumstances are willing to sacrifice their previous rights and to engage in thus far untried and novel ventures. The fact that what success there has been is along regional rather than world-wide lines indicates the importance of building on common interests and common understanding. The growing speed with which the West European integration movement is developing underscores the value of the vast amount of patient negotiation and detailed planning which goes into such endeavors.

So long, however, as nations seek salvation in power blocs and similar agglomerations, that is, in the concentration rather than the transfer of power, there is acute danger for all countries in a world of nations which are split ideologically and armed with weapons of destruction. It may be optimistic, but perhaps not utopian, to expect that this realization of both common dangers and common objectives will in the end prove stronger than the pull of fear and the urge toward power. In that event, international organization will have an impact on government and politics far greater than any other force in the world today.

IX

DEMOCRACY IN THE MODERN WORLD

Now that we have concluded this survey of some of the forces and problems which confront governments today, we are ready to return to two basic questions of central interest in this book: What is the essential nature of democracy and of totalitarianism? And how valid are the charges against democracy which were raised in the beginning of this book? In reaching our final conclusions on these matters, we must keep in mind that there are many states with a greater or lesser leaning toward democracy which are neither completely democratic nor totalitarian; that even liberal democracies are subject to strains of emotion, fear, and self-interest which sometimes lead them to adopt techniques or, temporarily, even objectives more characteristic of totalitarian dictatorships than they like to realize; and that in the world of today both the tasks and the organization of government are at all times complex, highly demanding, and absolutely vital to the future of any "modern" society.

THE TWO PATTERNS OF DEMOCRACY AND TOTALITARIANISM

Despite the strains and tensions to which democracies are subject, there remain certain clear differentiations between liberal democracy and totalitarian dictatorship or totalitarian oligarchy (in the sense of the terms as we have defined them in the beginning of this book) which are worth reiterating. As we have seen, in a totalitarian dictatorship the power exercised by its governing group is unlimited and unrestrained, and the authority of the regime extends into every aspect of the life of the individual. In a liberal democracy, in contrast, the exercise of political power is limited by a constitutional framework, or by convention, which protects certain areas of life from governmental interference and provides that the powers allowed the government shall be exercised according to known rules and procedures. The simplest distinction to be made between these two forms of government is thus between unlimited and limited government. As someone has said: "In democracies what is not forbidden is permitted; in dictatorships it is compulsory."

Behind these differences lie two sharply contrasting conceptions of the political community. The first, endorsed by both Communist and Nazi totalitarianisms, is that this community is an entity with a specific purpose of its own, which may be something quite different from the immediate purposes and desires of its members. This view is linked in turn to a belief in historical inevitability. Thus, the Soviet leaders, accepting the materialist conception of history, determine policy in the light of this (supposed) key to the future. In classical Marxism, of course, the state was stigmatized as an instrument of oppression used by the ruling class; Lenin envisioned it as an instrument of the working class in freeing itself from its oppressors. Stalin maintained that the Soviet state was a necessary protection of the working class against capitalist encirclement; and his successors continue to agree that it is the instrument for building the socialist society, which history (at least Marxist history) proves is the form of organization most in accord with advanced modes of economic production.

National Socialism similarly had its *Weltanschauung*, or world view, from which could be deduced the course of history. Its emphasis was on racialism, in contrast to the Marxist stress on economic determinism. But in the general view that the purposes of the organized political community have or should be given priority over those of the individuals who compose it, there is little difference between fascism and Marxism. Consequently, they both deny that there should be any limit on the exercise of political power on behalf of such a community.

Most advocates of liberal democracy, on the other hand, are not statists but believe in individualism. They do not deny that there may be meaning in history, but they insist that there is no *one* meaning, and that there is no inevitability in history—because they believe men have the opportunity to shape their own future within the limits provided by their experience and their environment. Thus, they point out that Marx's prophecies about the inevitable collapse of capitalism failed to materialize because, for one thing, people were forewarned by his prophecy and proceeded to take measures against the widening division between labor and capital that was taking place in his time. Instead of believing that the future is already determined by the conditions of the present, democratic thinkers maintain that man can use his intelligence to direct policies so as to modify, if not forestall, what may seem to be impending.

But if man can so act, it is a natural corollary that the state is controlled by individuals, and not that the state gives meaning to the lives of individuals. And at this point we return to the conception of limits which has been put forward as the characteristic feature of a democracy. For it is only when there are limits on what the government may do, and on the way in which it may do it, that the citizens are in control. In a mass society, the controls should ultimately be in the hands of the whole community, but within such a framework of limitations that the rights of individuals and of minorities are protected.

It is apparent that this definition of "liberal" democracy is different from the "plebiscitary" democracy, which, grounded in the ideas of Rousseau and the practices of the French Revolution, tends to give majorities the unlimited power to determine policies. Liberal democracy implies that even majorities must respect the basic spheres of individuals and of groups.

This means that the right of the individual to pursue his own spiritual and cultural life and the right of minorities to express their views freely and to influence policy are as much a part of democracy as popular control. It is for this reason that countries like Great Britain and France as well as the United States cherish civil liberties and that the opposition plays so vital a part in the British parliamentary process.

It has often been said, however, that only countries reared in a tradition of constitutionalism have respect for such limitations upon government. Nor can we deny that the countries in which Marxism and fascism have had the greatest effect are those which had the weakest constitutional tradition. Thus it seems clear that newly independent countries like India have a great initial handicap in establishing liberal democracy because of the slightness of their earlier constitutional tradition (and even India knows much more about constitutionalism because of its long contact with the British than do many other politically new countries). And yet, if the earlier argument has been correct, the essential requirements of democracy in these new countries, as in the older democracies, will be the acceptance of restraints on the operations of government and the willingness to follow empirical methods rather than an unrestrained rule that operates in terms of some preconceived or personally determined goal.

It is, however, necessary to be realistic about what is expected of a state under modern conditions. Beyond the traditional democratic demands of civil and political rights are the hopes and expectations encouraged by the material achievements of science and industrial technology as well as the requirements of modernization, made increasingly urgent by the population explosion, especially in the developing nations. And as scientific knowledge and technological possibilities expand, so does the sphere of political activity. Whatever is capable of organization and manipulation will ultimately come, to some degree at least, within the state's purview. All the more reason, therefore, to confront the actualities of politics and world affairs with the experimental spirit of science. While totalitarian leaders have often been hampered by their doctrinaire approach, the students and practitioners of politics in democratic states can be constantly searching for new ways to meet their problems, borrowing from others where it fits their needs and countering the dangers with which they are constantly confronted.

CAN LIBERAL DEMOCRACY WORK?

The charges against liberal democracy raised at the beginning, it may be remembered, were of two types. First are those that concern the machinery of democratic government—the instruments of information, the party system, representative institutions, and the making and administering of policy. But there are also questions that probe more deeply and raise the issue of whether the intellectual and moral qualities necessary for the successful functioning of liberal democracy are not lacking under modern conditions; whether the enormously increased responsibilities of government are not too numerous and complex for the comprehension of the ordinary citizen; and whether the conditions of economic strain, international conflict, and racial or group hostility have not destroyed the reasonableness, patience, and tolerance necessary for voluntary peaceful agreement.

The Machinery of Democracy Evaluated

When we look at those questions which concern the machinery of democratic governments and then reconsider the vast variety of institutional forms which exist, we realize that there is no such thing as a "democratic political machinery" in general. On the contrary, one of the greatest strengths of democracy is the abundant variety of devices and combinations of devices which can be used to achieve free, representative, responsible, and efficient government. There may be a two-party system or a multiparty system or even a more or less democratic one-party system; the parties themselves may be highly disciplined, loosely disciplined, or not disciplined at all—and the same party system may include several kinds of parties. Authority may be divided among the legislature, the cabinet, the party organizations, the civil service, the judiciary, or even extragovernmental groups in any number of possible combinations. The cabinet may be composed of one party or several, or even, as in the curious situation in Austria, of both major parties on a cartel-like basis of "parity." The legislature may have a clear party majority or a system that prevents any party from getting a majority. It may be elected in a great variety of ways, from the simple direct election of the House of Commons to the indirect election of the French Senate. There can be such anachronisms as the hereditary House of Lords, or the appointive system under which the Canadian Senate has traditionally operated. The legislature may have a set of specialized committees or a number of them which are unspecialized, and it may arrange its procedure so that ministers or high officials dominate the proceedings or so that private members assume the leadership. It may be under the threat of dissolution by the executive or have secure tenure, as do American legislatures, for the entire period between fixed elections.

The government itself may be under strong one-man leadership, as in the American Presidential system, or it may consist of a group of equals, among whom the prime minister is only somewhat "more equal than the others," as in the British cabinet system; or somewhere in between these two types, as in the West German chancellorship government. The government may administer a large number of public services directly, or it may use devices like the public corporation. Different degrees

of authority may be given to civil servants, who may be re-
cruited in a variety of ways and with a variety of qualifications
in mind. There is no necessary uniformity in the pattern of
local government or in the division of authority between national and local governments, or, where there is a federal structure, between the federation and its components. Even the
courts may follow the most divergent patterns of organization
and training. No single formula is obligatory. The very lack of
authoritarianism in principle encourages experiment and inventiveness.

Every country necessarily develops its own type of political
institutions in terms of its historical heritage, its social and economic institutions, and its ultimate objectives. Moreover, these
political institutions have their own coherence or inner logic.
Thus a powerful legislative committee system is not compatible with the strong executive of the British parliamentary
system, which works through its control of the House of Commons, while it is compatible with the powerful American executive, because the latter has its separate sphere of action. In
other words, no particular means of political action or political
control can be judged apart from its historical context and national setting. Moreover, no failure of one set of democratic
institutions on the mechanical level can be taken as proof of
the failure of democratic machinery in general.

At the same time, there are certain tests by which we can determine the health of a democracy. Is its constitutional framework of individual rights and recognized procedures jealously
safeguarded? Are its press and other channels of expression presenting as full and accurate information as possible, providing
a channel for the expression of all important political ideas,
and promoting the discussion which is essential for popular
participation in politics? Do its channels of political action operate to facilitate criticism, to enable minorities to differ from
the majority and to make their views heard with ease within

parties, parliament, and the country at large, and to ensure that at intervals the general policy of a government is passed upon by the voters in a general election? And is power, whether centered in political leaders, or parliaments, or a particular party, or even a particular group within the country, being exercised responsibly in the interests of the common good? In any nation in which some of these questions must be answered in the negative, one may seriously question whether democratic government can long endure.

The Assumption of Democracy Evaluated

Underlying these tests of the working of a democratic system are certain assumptions about human beings which do not go unchallenged. Many have questioned the capacity of people to understand the voluminous and technical problems of modern government; others suggest that war and economic strife have destroyed the qualities of character needed for peaceful agreement and compromise. It is clear that no governmental device can make men more intelligent or public-spirited or tolerant or reasonable than their own capacity and the conditions of modern life permit. The fundamental question for democracy today is whether, however adequate the machinery, human beings have the qualities of mind and character to make it function.

Fortunately, the attack on the capacities and character of the ordinary citizen is overly simple in some of its assumptions. The citizen does not have to be technically competent in every phase of governmental activity in order to judge whether or not he is well-governed. The political decisions required of him are relatively simple, and he is not ill-equipped to make them. As Aristotle noted, the person who eats a dinner is as good a judge of its quality as the cook. The citizen is concerned with purposes and results rather than the technical means of accomplishing them. It requires a technician to plan and build a bridge, but it is the citizen who knows better than anyone else his own desires and needs, and he is better equipped than anyone else to tell whether his government is satisfying them.

The Western democracies have provided us with considerable evidence that an educated and experienced electorate is not a bad judge of the important issues of modern politics. There have been encouraging signs of restraint and judgment from some of the newer Asian and African states like India, the Philippines, Nigeria, and Zambia. Certainly those prophets who expected the extension of the suffrage to result in a tide of reckless and revolutionary legislation have been badly disappointed. Even in foreign relations, where the judgment of the ordinary citizen would seem most badly handicapped by lack of personal knowledge and experience, the policy of the older and newer democracies has never been so disastrous as that of a Hitler or a Mussolini; and there is some reason for believing that the leaders of the Soviet Union, despite their reputation for Machiavellian cunning, have not been more accurate in their assessment of political realities than have democratic statesmen—and have made as many blunders, if not more.

In fact, a survey of modern governments suggests that some of those observers who have been most ruthless in their assessment of the political incapacity of the people have been most credulous in their willingness to attribute supernatural qualities of wisdom and integrity to the leaders and administrators of authoritarian states. Yet, revelations of the nature of Hitler and his "court" disclose a degree of folly of which no democracy has shown itself capable. Similarly, it would be hard to think of a more devastating indictment of Soviet leadership than the revelations about Stalin made by the Soviet's own succeeding top leadership.

If one turns from the question of technical competence to

that of the moral preconditions for successful democratic government—calmness, reasonableness, and patience in arriving at
decisions; a desire to come to peaceful agreement and, therefore, a willingness to make concessions and compromises; a
feeling of confidence that no political group will attempt to
impose its will by force, or use violent means to keep other
groups from attaining power, or overthrow the constitutional
system—it seems clear that such qualities are not easily and
quickly acquired, but rather are fostered by long experience
and, in general, by favorable economic, social, and even geographical circumstances. Where such qualities and experience
are lacking, the establishment of democracy is, at best, difficult;
it is significant that in countries like Great Britain and the
United States, where democracy has been most successful, children are taught from their earliest schooldays to play the game,
accept defeat with good sportsmanship and victory with gener-
osity, abide by the will of the majority, and take criticism and
disagreement in good part. In fact, the very success with which
these qualities are inculcated in the democracies—the belief
that any problem can be solved if only men of good will meet
each other in reasonable discussion around a table—has made
it difficult for their leaders to understand and deal with those
representatives of authoritarian governments who, like Hitler
before World War II or Communist leaders today, cannot
think in terms of enduring compromise but only in terms of
total victory and crushing defeat; who regard concessions as a
sign of weakness and a compromise not as an enduring agreement but rather as a resting place on the road to the complete
achievement of their original aims; who look forward to crushing their enemies, and who cannot conceive of tolerating a
"loyal opposition."

But more than education is necessary for the cultivation of
the political attitudes that democratic government requires.
Democracy flourishes best where there is a feeling of economic

well-being and security. He who lives under conditions of civil strife or violence is all too likely to consider order—even when brought about by a strong man—preferable to the uncertainty and the risks of a freer existence. The man who suffers from grinding poverty and the anxieties of unemployment finds it difficult to be detached and reasonable in his judgments, to weigh judiciously the fate of the commonwealth while his children go hungry. It is here that the nations of the world face the greatest problems of the final decades of this century. The rising and rapidly growing masses of the world's "south," the "proletariat" of the present-day world, will hardly be able to achieve the maturity liberal democracy requires without a rapid improvement in living standards; if the poor nations are not lifted out of their present squalor, their governments, whether democratic or not, are likely to fall into anarchy, and the great powers may be pulled into the vortex. Therefore, it is not only a matter of moral concern but also of self-interest for the advanced nations of the "north" to lend whatever assistance they can to the development of the poor. Moreover, in their own countries, the "affluent" know still all too many pockets of poverty, often connected with racial discrimination (as in the case of the American Negro). But, as his example has shown so vividly, desire for human dignity does not cease even under conditions of misery and discrimination. The same is true of many of the peoples of color who have recently emerged or are emerging to nationhood. And nowhere does desire for freedom flourish more glowingly than where it is temporarily suppressed by totalitarian controls. To this the Hungarian people testified when rising against oppressive rule. The "thaw" which has since set in in Hungary as well as in other former Soviet "satellites" despite outward failure of revolutions affords reason to hope that the cause of freedom is not lost as long as people cherish a feeling of what it means and a desire to attain or retrieve it.

The democratic way of political life is not an easy one, but its rewards are great. No form of government is simpler than that of one man ruling over others; yet all history stands as a record of the abuse of power so concentrated. Democracy requires from its citizens a level of political intelligence, experience, maturity, public spirit, and self-restraint which is lacking in large parts of the world; and it also demands the exercise of ingenuity in finding solutions and developing the political machinery appropriate for a system which desires freedom and responsibility as well as efficiency. The great strength of democracy is that its way of life fosters and encourages these very qualities. It is in the democracies that no one attitude or solution is orthodox, that diversity and experiment are considered natural and desirable. And as one looks at the great variety of devices which have in practice been developed for the realization of democratic aims, it would be rash to conclude that in imaginativeness, willingness to experiment, and social idealism, the democracies yield in any way to other forms of government.

SELECTED BIBLIOGRAPHY

ALMOND, GABRIEL A., and COLEMAN, JAMES S. *The Politics of the Developing Areas.* Princeton, N.J.: Princeton University Press; London: Oxford University Press, 1960.

ALMOND, GABRIEL A., and VERBA, SIDNEY. *The Civic Culture: Political Attitudes in Five Nations.* Princeton, N.J.: Princeton University Press, 1963.

ANDREWS, WILLIAM G. (ed.). *Constitutions and Constitutionalism.* (2nd ed.). Princeton, N.J.: D. Van Nostrand Co., 1963, paperback.

ARENDT, HANNAH. *The Origins of Totalitarianism.* (2nd enl. ed.) New York: Meridian Books, 1958.

BERRINGTON, HUGH. *How Nations Are Governed.* New York: Pitman Publishing Corp., 1965.

BOWIE, ROBERT R., and FRIEDRICH, CARL J. *Studies in Federalism.* Boston: Little Brown and Company, 1954.

BRIMMEL, J. H. *Communism in South East Asia: A Political Analysis.* New York and London: Oxford University Press for the Royal Institute of International Affairs, 1959.

BROGAN, D. W. *Citizenship Today: England-France-the United States.* Chapel Hill, N.C.: University of North Carolina Press, 1960.

————, and VERNEY, DOUGLAS V. *Political Patterns in Today's World.* New York: Harcourt, Brace & World, 1962, paperback.

BRYCE, VISCOUNT JAMES. *Modern Democracies.* 2 vols. New York and London: The Macmillan Company, 1921.

CARTER, GWENDOLEN M. (ed.). *African One-Party States.* Ithaca, N.Y.: Cornell University Press, 1962.

————. *Five African States: Responses to Diversity.* Ithaca, N.Y.: Cornell University Press, 1963.

————, and WESTIN, ALAN (eds.). *Politics in Europe.* New York: Harcourt, Brace & World, 1965.

CASTBERG, FREDE. *Freedom of Speech in the West: A Comparative Study of Public Law.* Dobbs Ferry, N.Y.: Oceana Publications; London: Allen & Unwin, 1960.

CHAMBERS, WILLIAM N., and SALISBURY, ROBERT H. (eds.). *Democracy in the Mid-Twentieth Century: Problems and Prospects,* St. Louis, Mo.: Washington University Press, 1960.

CHAPMAN, BRIAN. *The Profession of Government: The Public Service in Europe.* New York: The Macmillan Company; London: Allen & Unwin, 1959.

CHRISTOPH, JAMES B. (ed.). *Cases in Comparative Politics.* Boston: Little, Brown and Company, 1965, paperback.

COLEMAN, JAMES S., and ROSBERG, CARL (eds.). *Political Parties and National Integration in Tropical Africa.* Berkeley and Los Angeles: University of California Press, 1965.

DUVERGER, MAURICE. *Political Parties: Their Organization and Activity in the Modern State.* Translated by BARBARA and ROBERT NORTH, New York: John Wiley & Sons; London: Methuen & Co., 1954.

EHRMANN, HENRY W. (ed.). *Interest Groups on Four Continents.* Pittsburgh, Pa.: University of Pittsburgh Press, 1958.

————. *Democracy in a Changing Society.* New York: Frederick A. Praeger, 1965.

EINAUDI, MARIO, and GOGUEL, FRANÇOIS. *Communism in Western Europe.* Ithaca, N.Y.: Cornell University Press, 1951.

FINER, HERMAN. *The Theory and Practice of Modern Government.* (4th ed.). New York: Holt, Rinehart and Winston; London: Methuen & Co., 1961.

FINER, S. E. *The Man on Horseback: The Role of the Military in Politics.* New York: Frederick A. Praeger; London: Pall Mall Press, 1962.

FRIEDMAN, W. (ed.). *The Public Corporation: A Comparative Symposium.* Toronto: Carswell Company; London: Stevens & Sons, 1954.

FRIEDRICH, CARL J. *Constitutional Government and Democracy; Theory and Practice in Europe and America* (rev. ed.). Boston: Ginn & Company, 1960.

————, and BRZEZINSKI, ZBIGNIEW K. *Totalitarian Dictatorship and Autocracy* (2nd rev. ed.). Cambridge, Mass.: Harvard University Press, 1965.

GEERTZ, CLIFFORD (ed.). *Old Societies and New States: A Quest for Modernity in Asia and Africa.* New York: The Free Press of Glencoe, 1963.

HANNA, WILLIAM J., and HANNA, JUDY (eds.). *Independent Black Africa.* Chicago: Rand McNally, 1965.

HERZ, JOHN. *International Politics in the Atomic Age.* New York: Columbia University Press, 1960.

————. *Political Realism and Political Idealism: A Study in Theories and Realities.* Chicago: University of Chicago Press, 1951.

JANOWITZ, MORRIS. *The Military in the Political Development of the New Nations.* Chicago: University of Chicago Press, 1964.

KIRCHHEIMER, OTTO. *Political Justice.* Princeton, N.J.: Princeton University Press, 1961.

LAKEMAN, ENID, and LAMBERT, JAMES D. *Voting in Democracies* (rev. ed.). New York: Hillary House Publishers; London: Faber & Faber, 1955.

LAPALOMBARA, JOSEPH (ed.). *Bureaucracy and Political Development.* Princeton, N.J.: Princeton University Press, 1963.

LOEWENSTEIN, KARL. *Political Power and the Governmental Process.* Chicago: University of Chicago Press, 1965, paperback.

MACIVER, ROBERT M. *The Web of Government.* New York: The Macmillan Company, 1947.

MACRIDIS, ROY C., and BROWN, BERNARD E. *Comparative Politics: Notes and Readings* (rev. ed.). Homewood, Ill.: The Dorsey Press, 1965.

NEUMANN, SIGMUND (ed.). *Modern Political Parties: Approaches to Comparative Politics.* Chicago: University of Chicago Press; London: Cambridge University Press, 1958.

PEASLEE, AMOS J. *Constitutions of the Nations.* 3 vols. (2nd ed.). New York: Justice House, 1965.

POST, K. W. J. *The New States of West Africa.* Baltimore: Penguin Africa Library, 1964.

ROSSITER, CLINTON LAWRENCE. *Constitutional Dictatorship: Crisis Government in the Modern Democracies.* Princeton, N.J.: Princeton University Press; London: Oxford University Press, 1948.

SCHMITT, KARL M., and BURKS, DAVID D. *Evolution or Chaos: Dynamics of Latin American Government and Politics.* New York: Frederick A. Praeger, 1963.

SMITH, T. E. *Elections in Developing Countries.* New York: St. Martin's Press, 1960.

SPIRO, HERBERT J. *Government by Constitution.* New York: Random House, 1959.

STAMPS, NORMAN L. *Why Democracies Fail: A Critical Evaluation of the Causes of Modern Dictatorship.* Notre Dame, Ind.: University of Notre Dame Press, 1957.

WHEARE, KENNETH C. *Legislatures.* New York and London: Oxford University Press, 1963, paperback.

————. *Federal Government* (4th ed.). New York and London: Oxford University Press, 1964, paperback.

————. *Modern Constitutions.* New York and London: Oxford University Press, 1951.